Preface and Acknowledgements

Since the founding of Jamestown, Virginia, and its westward expansion, there has always been trials and tribulations. From the working class to the upper class, no one was exempt from the challenges of frontier life. Even though they faced different obstacles, they would eventually overcome them to contribute to Virginia history.

These narratives, largely based on less well-known pioneers, is the foundation for this book. By examining their lives, it is my hope the readers of these genealogical adventures will learn about the history of colonial Virginia.

I want to give my sincere thanks to March Conrad, Ruth Stanley Kuntz, and Darlene Stanley of the National Stanley Family Association for their generous assistance. I also wish to thank Debra Joyce for painting the book cover, and Thomas Joyce, James Webster, and Joyce Wells Lawrence for editing.

David C Joyce

Introduction

The narratives portrayed in this book represent the life stories of various pioneers from eighteenth-century Virginia. Their struggles and achievements are not well-known; nevertheless, they played a crucial role. From poor immigrants, religious dissenters, and the landed gentry, they all changed Virginia history.

Crucial to the development of the Colony of Virginia is how the working class lived. Often arriving as indentured servants or poor immigrants, they had to work their way up in society. Michael Kelly, the subject of chapter 2, is a prime example of this. Taking jobs that no one else wanted, he helped form the economic and political foundation in Virginia.

Closely related to the contributions of the working class was how refugees shaped society. During the early eighteenth-century, Scots-Irish settlers, like Thomas Joyce in chapter 6, immigrated to Virginia for a better life. Their stories, shrouded in political and religious persecution, ultimately forced colonial society to accept religious freedom.

Chapter 7 examines the life of Thomas Stanley, a member of the Society of Friends. Like Thomas Joyce, Thomas Stanley experienced political and religious persecution but to a larger degree. Focused on the culture of the Quakers, this chapter also examines how they survived.

Also of worthy of examination is how the upper class influenced and governed the colony. Entrepreneurs like Charles Chiswell in chapter 1 supported the economy while offering employment to immigrants. A progressive businessman, his efforts made him a respected figure.

Similar to the narrative of Charles Chiswell is the account of Nicholas Meriwether in chapter 3. One of the largest landowners in central Virginia, he managed to rise in social status and in political influence. Through his endeavors, he assisted in successfully governing the Virginia colony, so much so, that he rose to the highest level in government.

However, not every settler made a positive contribution to society. Chapter 5 describes the life of Sir Francis Wyatt, the first Royal Governor of Virginia. Involved in a bitter dispute between the Queen of the Pamunkey, leader of the Native American tribes, he went to extreme measures to protect Jamestown. He would also be a key character in preserving the General Assembly, the self-governing legislature body in Virginia.

Opposite Sir Francis Wyatt, chapter 4 discuss the struggles of the Queen of the Pamunkey. Tasked with saving her tribe from starvation, disease, and a declining population, she also proved to be a skillful politician. Successfully manipulating the English political system for the benefit of her people, she proved to be a formable enemy.

Chapter 8 discusses the accomplishments of William Witcher, a soldier and politician from the working class. An active member of his community, he preserved and protected its interests from aggressive Native Americans and the British. Politically, he became one of the most influential men in Pittsylvania County, Virginia.

All of these pioneers, in their own way, contributed to the culture of colonial Virginia. For better or for worse, they either inspired hope or planted fear. In some cases, it was both. The history of Virginia was shaped forever by these pioneers and their decisions.

Chapter 1
Charles Chiswell

The growth of the eighteenth-century economy driven in-part by wealthy gentlemen, was an important part of our nation's history. The new world attracted adventurous frontiersmen, businessmen, and land speculators, and, as such, was bound to evolve. In addition to the working class that helped expand the colony, one cannot overlook the work done by the wealthy planters. Not waiting for new land to be explored, merchants and politicians were granted large land grants. With the hope of selling it or planting tobacco, the crash crop of Virginia, they could easily become rich.

One such person, Charles Chiswell, became an important figure within the chronicles of colonial Virginia. Said to be an immigrant from Scotland, he worked his way up the political hierarchy by investing in land. The builder of the Scotchtown plantation, the birthplace of Patrick Henry,[1] he was also active in the mining industry.[2] Due to the activities of such men, the history of Virginia is not complete without their contributions.

Charles Chiswell: Said to be born in Scotland; died on April 8, 1737 in Williamsburg, Virginia[3]. He married Esther Chiswell.[4]

---

[1] Richmond, Virginia, National Register of Historic Places Inventory – Nomination Form: 2, "Scotchtown," December 21, 1965; digital image, Virginia Department of Historic Resources: accessed August 15, 2106; Richard N. Côté, *Strength and Honor: The Life of Dolley Madison* (Mount Pleasant, South Carolina: Corinthian Books, 2005), 44.

[2] Randal L. Hall, *Mountains on the Market: Industry, the Environment, and the South* (Lexington, Kentucky: The University Press of Kentucky, 2012), 14.

[3] Preservation Virginia, *Preservation Virginia* (https://preservationvirginia.org/: accessed 3 July 2017), "Patrick Henry's Scotchtown."; *Personal Notices from the Virginia Gazette, the William and Mary Quarterly*, (Williamsburg, Virginia: Omohundro Institute of Early American History and Culture, April 1897), 241, JSTOR (http://www.jstor.org/stable/1914927: accessed August 5, 2017).

[4] Preservation Virginia, *Preservation Virginia*, "Patrick Henry's Scotchtown."

Charles's Parentage: His parents are not known; however, according to the histories of the Chiswell family, he emigrated from Scotland. This occurred sometime before 1704.[5]

Life Story: Appearing as Clerk of the General Court on December 15, 1704, Charles Chiswell had already begun to ascend to the highest level of society.[6] How he obtained this appointment is not documented; however, this position allowed him to become a crucial part of the government.

As clerk, Charles Chiswell organized the minutes for the general court. A witness to the approval of land grants, he gained invaluable insight into how the economy functioned. On December 24, 1714, Charles and Frederick Jones requested that, "*a Patient [be] issue[d] in their name for four thousand one hundred & fifty acres lying in New Kent County*" be processed and approved.[7] His role as a member of the Governor's Council taught him how to earn income and rise in social status.

Virginia in 1714 was an unexplored frontier and provided men like Charles a way to benefit financially. The purpose of following these endeavors depended on the viewpoint of the land speculator. If you were a government official, you wanted to earn income for yourself, the colony, and to expand trade routes. Trusted by his fellow council members, he received his first land grant in 1714. If a petitioner for land "*was not known to any of the board [council],*" then "*[this quality is] thought too much for so obscure a person.*"[8]

Economically and politically, Charles Chiswell benefited from his business deals. On October 17, 1716, he is documented as "*Erecting therefore a Storehouse and Wharf for his greater Conveniency in*

---

[5] H. R. Mcilwaine, *Executive Journals of the Council of Colonial Virginia: Volume 2* (Richmond, Virginia: The Virginia State Library, 1927), 448.

[6] Mcilwaine, *Executive Journals of the Council of Colonial Virginia: Volume 3*, (Richmond, Virginia: The Virginia State Library), 394.

[7] Mcilwaine, *Executive Journals of the Council of Colonial Virginia: Volume 2*, (Richmond, Virginia: The Virginia State Library, 1927), 448.

[8] Warren R. Hofstra, *The Planting of New Virginia* (Baltimore and London: The John Hopkins University Press, 2004), 55, *Google Books* (http://www.books.google.com: accessed 5 August 2017).

Victualing His Maj^{tys} Ships of War according to his Contract."[9] Working with the English Crown, he pursued land speculation as a career.

On July 15, 1717, Charles is granted 9,976 acres in New Kent County, Virginia.[10] His motivation was for economic gain, and this led to the construction of Scotchtown. [11]

Building his home on this property, he named it Scotchtown to attract Scottish workers.[12] An entrepreneur, he anticipated these Scotsmen building, *"mills, laundries, blacksmith shops, and even a castle."*[13] However, due to an epidemic of yellow fever, the workers left the planation and returned back to Scotland.[14] By 1732, he finally achieved success and established the Fredericksville Company, an Iron works, in Hanover County.[15]

Charles Chiswell not only used land grants to help the government, but he also had an interest in earning money. As frontier families moved further west, Charles was aware that they needed land on which to live. In anticipation of this, by June 20, 1733, he acquired 29,085 acres of land in Hanover County,[16] 21, 568

---

[9] Warren R. Hofstra, *The Planting of New Virginia* (Baltimore and London: The John Hopkins University Press, 2004), 430, *Google Books* (http://www.books.google.com: accessed 5 August 2017).

[10] "Online Catalog: Images & indexes," database with images, *The Library of Virginia* (http://lva1.hosted.exlibrisgroup.com: accessed 5 August 2017), Charles Chiswell, 15 July 1717, 9976 acres, Virginia, Colonial Land Office, Patents, 1623-1774; Library of Virginia.

[11] Richmond, Virginia, National Register of Historic Places Inventory – Nomination Form: 2, "Scotchtown," December 21, 1965; digital image, Virginia Department of Historic Resources: accessed August 15 2106; Preservation Virginia, *Preservation Virginia*, "Patrick Henrys Scotchtown."

[12] Richmond, Virginia, National Register of Historic Places Inventory – Nomination Form: 2, "Scotchtown."

[13] Dale Page Talley, *Hanover County* (Charleston, South Carolina: Arcadia Publishing, 2004).

[14] Talley, *Hanover County.*

[15] Richmond, Virginia, National Register of Historic Places Inventory – Nomination Form: 2, "Scotchtown."

[16] "Online Catalog: Images & indexes," database with images, *The Library of Virginia* (http://lva1.hosted.exlibrisgroup.com: accessed 6 August 2017), Charles Chiswell, 21 November 1727, 742 acres, 28 September 1728,4975 acres; 25 August 1731, 15, 568 acres; 20 June 1733, 400 acres, Virginia, Colonial Land Office, Patents, 1623-1774; Library of Virginia; H. R. Mcilwaine, *Executive Journals of the Council of Colonial Virginia: Volume 4* (Richmond, Virginia: The Virginia State Library, 1927), 83, 128, 179, 258.

acres in Spotsylvania County,[17] and 2,000 in Henrico County.[18] As a land speculator, he felt inclined to sell these families land on which to build a home. This allowed more frontiersmen to explore new lands to the west.

Another avenue he pursued was growing tobacco and flax seed. The quality and prices of tobacco fluctuated, but it always remained a valuable commodity. As a wealthy merchant, Charles Chiswel had the opportunity to sell tobacco with markets in England and Virginia.

The ability to plant, grow, and harvest tobacco depended on a large labor force. By the time Charles is documented as receiving land grants, indentured servants had declined in number due to an influx of African Slaves. As a result, planters could procure cheap labor.

The knowledge Charles acquired as Clerk of the General Court was not exclusively based on land speculation. As part of the inner circle of high society, he also witnessed the appointment of justices of the peace and sheriffs. Important to the security of Virginia, these offices were an essential part of frontier society. Privy to this and other workings of the Governor's Council, he earned the right to receive land grants.

Ironically, Charles Chiswell's death was also closely related to this enterprise. Around the time when he was first granted 4,150 acres in 1714,[19] he probably already had a son, John Chiswell,[20] and a girl, Mary

[17] "Online Catalog: Images & indexes," database with images, *The Library of Virginia* (http://lva1.hosted.exlibrisgroup.com: accessed 6 August 2017), Charles Chiswell, 28 September 1728, 1000 acres; 25 August 1731, 15, 568 acres, Virginia, Colonial Land Office, Patents, 1623-1774; Library of Virginia; H. R. Mcilwaine, *Executive Journals of the Council of Colonial Virginia: Volume 4* (Richmond, Virginia: The Virginia State Library, 1927), 258.

[18] H. R. Mcilwaine, *Executive Journals of the Council of Colonial Virginia: Volume 4* (Richmond, Virginia: The Virginia State Library, 1927), 26.

[19] Mcilwaine, *Executive Journals of the Council of Colonial Virginia: Volume 4*, 83.

[20] Philip Alexander Bruce, William Glover Stanard, *The Virginia Magazine of History and Biography: Vol 4* (Virginia: Virginia Historical Society, 1896), 359, *Google Books* (http://www.books.google.com: accessed 7 April 2017).

Chiswell,[21] by his wife, Esther. After Charles passed away in 1737, John Chiswell inherited his father's lands and the Fredericksville Company.[22] It was often that sons of wealthy gentlemen inherited their father's income and land. Besides taking up political office, this was how men like Charles Chiswell kept their legacy alive.

Children

The Children of Charles Chiswell and Ether (?) are as follows:

- Captain John Chiswell, born in Virginia, likely around 1715; died October 14, 1766 in Williamsburg, Virginia.[23] He married Elizabeth Randolph.[24]
- Mary Chiswell, born in Virginia, likely born around 1715. She married Charles Barrett.[25]

Conclusion

The successful expansion of the Virginia Colony, due to the efforts of frontier families, was also accomplished with the help of land speculators. While explorers adventured into unknown parts, speculators contributed to this by buying recently discovered territories. One of these gentlemen, Charles Chiswell, was a prominent planter and has left a detailed genealogical record. Purchasing vast amounts of land, he expanded the limits of central Virginia while also establishing

---

[21] William Byrd, Louis Wright, Marion Tinling, *The Secret Diary of William Byrd of Westover, 1709-1712* (Richmond, Virginia: The Dietz Press, 1941), 99, *Hathitrust* (https://www.hathitrust.org/: accessed 7 April 2017).

[22] Philip Alexander Bruce, William Glover Stanard, *The Virginia Magazine of History and Biography: Vol 4*, 359; Lyon Gardiner Tyler, Richard Lee Morton, The William and Mary Quarterly, Volume 22 (Richmond, Virginia: Whittet & Shepperson, Printers, 1914), 59, *Google Books* (http://www.books.google.com/: accessed 7 August 2017).

[23] Virginia Armstead Garber, *The Armstead Family: 1635-1910* (Richmond, Virginia: Whittet & Shepperson, Printers, 1910), 61, *Google Books* (http://www.books.google.com: accessed 7 August 2017).

[24] Virginia Armstead Garber, *The Armstead Family: 1635-1910* (Richmond, Virginia: Whittet & Shepperson, Printers, 1910), 56, *Google Books* (http://www.books.google.com: accessed 7 August 2017).

[25] Byrd, Wright, Tinling, *The Secret Diary of William Byrd of Westover, 1709-1712*, 99.

an iron works. A much loved figure in colonial Virginia, he left a lasting legacy. [26]

- On December 15, 1704, Charles Chiswell is recorded as being Clerk of the General Court of Virginia. Closely associated with the Governor's Council, he was part of an exclusive, inner-circle
- Tasked with organizing and documenting the minutes of the Governor's Council, Charles gained invaluable insight into high society. A witness to the procedures of the council, he kept track of who received land grants, who was appointed justices, and other important issues.

- On December 24, 1714, Charles Chiswell received a land grant *"for four thousand one hundred & fifty acres lying in New Kent County. "*[27] By June 20, 1733, he had acquired 62, 629 acres of land.[28]
- An entrepreneur in his own right, he a built a *"Storehouse and Wharf for his greater Conveniency in Victualing His Maj^{tys} Ships of War according to his Contract."*[29] This indicates he had a business relationship with the English Crown.

- By 1732, he established an iron works, the Fredericksville Company, in Hanover and Spotsylvania County, Virginia.[30]
- Anticipating to build, *"mills, Laundries, blacksmith shops, and even a castle,"*[31] on the 9, 976 acres he purchased on 15 July 1717,[32] he planned to establish a community of Scottish workers. Naming this plantation, Scotchtown, an epidemic of

[26] Mcilwaine, *Executive Journals of the Council of Colonial Virginia: Volume 2*, 448.

[27] Mcilwaine, *Executive Journals of the Council of Colonial Virginia: Volume 2*, 448.

[28] Mcilwaine, *Executive Journals of the Council of Colonial Virginia: Volume 2*, 448; Online Catalog: Images & indexes," *The Library of Virginia* Charles Chiswell, 21 November 1727, 742 acres, 28 September 1728,4975 acres; 25 August 1731, 15, 568 acres; 20 June 1733, 400 acres, Virginia, Colonial Land Office, Patents, 1623-1774, Virginia, Colonial Land Office, Patents, 1623-1774; H. R. Mcilwaine, *Executive Journals of the Council of Colonial Virginia: Volume 4* , 26, 83, 128, 179, 258; "Online Catalog: Images & indexes," *The Library of Virginia*, Charles Chiswell, 28 September 1728, 1000 acres; 25 August 1731, 15, 568 acres, Virginia, Colonial Land Office, Patents, 1623-1774.

[29] Hofstra, *The Planting of New Virginia*, 430.

[30] Tyler, Morton, The William and Mary Quarterly, Volume 22, 59.

[31] Talley, *Hanover County*.

[32] "Online Catalog: Images & indexes", *The Library of Virginia*, Charles Chiswell, 15 July 1717, 9976 acres, Virginia, Colonial Land Office, Patents, 1623-1774.

yellow fever broke out, forcing these workers to return to Scotland.[33]

- Using indentured servants and African slaves, he grew tobacco, on his properties to sell locally and overseas.
- He also sold some of his land to frontier families who moved further west.

---

[33] Talley, *Hanover County*; Richmond, Virginia, National Register of Historic Places Inventory – Nomination Form: 2, "Scotchtown."

Chapter 2

Michael Kelly

The history of eighteenth-century Virginia is filled with stories of famous American patriots such as George Washington and Thomas Jefferson. However, despite their influence, they were not the true backbone of the colony.

Workers and farmers of all ethnic backgrounds, especially the Scots-Irish, were influential as well. While the wealthy were buying vast amounts of land to build their political and economic careers, the Scots-Irish were part of a society based on inequality. Importing themselves into Virginia or coming in as indentured servants, they had to work for everything. From herding cattle, growing their own crops, becoming soldiers, and even catching runaway slaves for income, they were true frontiersmen[1]

Michael Kelly, a Scots-Irish immigrant, imported himself from Ireland to Virginia in 1753.[2] On his arrival, he had little money and had to do the dirty jobs that only the working class accepted. Leaving his homeland due to famine, political upheaval, and a declining linen industry, he left Ireland with hope for a better life. By the end of his lifetime, he had created a stable life for himself and his family.

---

[1] Lyman Chalkley, *Chronicles of the Scotch-Irish Settlement in Virginia, Volume 1*, Kindle edition (The Commonwealth Printing Company: 1912); Larry J Hoefling, *Scots and Scotch Irish: Frontier Life in North Carolina, Virginia, And Kentucky* (Oklahoma: Inlandia Press, 2009), 151; Orange County, Virginia, Order Book. 6 (1754-1763): 36, Michael Kelly; Microfilm 32; Library of Virginia, Richmond.

[2] Orange County, Virginia, Order Book. No 5 (1747-1754): 36, Michael Kelly; Microfilm 32; Library of Virginia, Richmond.

Michael Kelly: Born before 1753 in Ireland; died about 1794, probably in Patrick County, Virginia. He married Mary Thompson on April 26, 1772 in Bedford County, Virginia.[3]

Michael's Parentage: Born in Ireland to unknown parents, Michael immigrated to the new world due to political and economic instability. It is unknown how Michael paid for his passage to Virginia; however, since the majority of immigrants were poor, there is a possibility he had financial support from his relatives.

Life Story: The story of Michael Kelly is rooted in the controversial history of the Scots-Irish. Born and raised in eighteenth-century Ireland, he witnessed religious and political persecutions. During his childhood, Northern Ireland was experiencing an economic depression because of oppressive trade policies, including an act that restricted woolen products to be traded only to England and Wales.[4]

With the income of the wool weavers reduced, they could not afford to pay their rent.[5] Michael's family probably suffered this same fate under this system of landlords. Farmers, too, were affected negatively. With Irish families unable to pay their rent, selling their crops also became ineffective as a source of income, especially when famine was destroying their food supply.[6] Michael's personal experience from this period of Irish history is unknown; however, he probably experienced starvation on a daily basis.[7]

Michael Kelly's interaction with the political and social upheaval in Northern Ireland had a troubling history as well. Founded on the discrimination against protestant dissenters, in 1704 the Established

---

[3] Rowland D. Buford, *Marriage Bonds of Bedford County, Virginia, 1755-1800* (Baltimore, Maryland: Genealogical Publishing Co., 38.

[4] Wayland F. Dunaway, *The Scotch-Irish of Colonial Pennsylvania* (1944; reprint, Baltimore, Maryland: Genealogical Publishing Co, Inc, 2002), 29.

[5] Dunaway, *The Scotch-Irish of Colonial Pennsylvania, 29.*

[6] Dunaway, *The Scotch-Irish of Colonial Pennsylvania, 29;* Wayland F. Dunaway, *The Scotch-Irish of Colonial Pennsylvania* (1944; reprint, Baltimore, Maryland: Genealogical Publishing Co, Inc, 2002), 30.

[7] Wayland F. Dunaway, *The Scotch-Irish of Colonial Pennsylvania* (1944; reprint, Baltimore, Maryland: Genealogical Publishing Co, Inc, 2002), 29.

Church of England implemented the Test Act.[8] Afraid of the nonconformists' influence, the English Church prohibited any dissenter from taking public office. To do so, they had to take communion as part of the Church of England. To reinforce this injustice, protestant dissenters were forced to pay tithes to the established church. The controversies did not end here, Michael's childhood memories also centered on the condemnation of the construction of Presbyterian Churches and declaring Presbyterian marriages illegal. The faith of Michael is not known; however, based on the year he immigrated to the new world, he likely was a protestant dissenter.

In 1753 Michael Kelly is first documented as having arrived in Orange County, Virginia.[9] At this time, he was a young adult and faced a difficult decision upon his arrival. Having paid for his passage to Virginia, he had the right of 50 acres of land, but in truth, he could not maintain it by himself.[10] As part of the working class, he did not have any slaves or indentured servants to work for him. One can imagine the regret, anger, and frustration when he was left with no choice but to give his land to John Bramham.[11] When he had finally arrived in a country of new opportunity and freedom, he was left with nothing.

Like other newly arrived Scots-Irish immigrants who had little money and possessions, Michael's struggle had only began. With no support system in the colonies, he had to build a life for himself, both socially and economically. The whereabouts of how and where he lived in Orange County is unknown. However, in August of 1754, he is in court where he is returning a runaway slave to John Spokwood under the certificate of Jeremiah Morton.[12]

---

[8] Wayland F. Dunaway, *The Scotch-Irish of Colonial Pennsylvania* (1944; reprint, Baltimore, Maryland: Genealogical Publishing Co, Inc, 2002), 31.

[9] Orange County, Virginia, Order Book. No 5: 36, microfilm 32.

[10] John A. Grigg, Peter C. Mancall, British Colonial America: People and Perspectives (Santa Barbara, California: ABC Clio, 2008), 239; digital images, *Google books* (http://www.books.google.com: accessed 25 December 2016).

[11] Orange County, Virginia, Order Book. No 5: 36, microfilm 32.

[12] Orange County, Virginia, Order Book. No 6: 36, microfilm 32.

The relationship between Michael Kelly and Jeremiah Morton is unknown, but Michael Kelly understood the importance of accepting any work he could. In August of 1754, he was added to the tithable list of the local parish.[13] By now, Michael had learned the new world wasn't what he thought it would be. His request to join the tithable list wasn't by choice since everyone, regardless of their religion was required to become part of the church. If Presbyterians, or any protestant dissenters, did not attend church services or did not pay tithes to their parish, their tithes were taxed.[14]

One year later in 1755, the nature of Michael's job had changed to husbandry. Living in nearby Augusta County, Virginia, he was now tasked with working with cattle in a Scots-Irish community.[15] Preferring the company of his fellow countrymen, he felt some sense of comfort. Augusta County had become a refuge for the Scots-Irish who migrated from Pennsylvania for land opportunities. Unlike the larger English settlements in Orange County, Augusta was situated on the frontier where the only laws were the customs of the inhabitants.

Michael's involvement with his community wasn't always on the best of terms. Although, he provided a valuable service by herding cattle and earned income from his work, he was known as a rabble-rouser. In May 1762, he was paid £1, 15 for driving cattle for 20 days, but then on February 18, 1761, he received twenty-five lashes for *"taking a horse without a press warrant"*.[16]

Despite this tainted relationship with his Scots-Irish neighbors, Michael also served in the militia to protect his community. Living on the outskirts of civilization required organized

---

[13] Orange County, Virginia, Order Book. No 5: 37, microfilm 32.

[14] Robert P. Davis, James H. Smylie, Dean K. Thompson, Ernest Trice Thompson, William Newton Todd, *Virginia Presbyterians in American Life: Hanover Presbytery (1755-1980)* (Richmond, Virginia: Hanover Presbytery, 1982), 5.

[15] Lyman Chalkley, *Chronicles of the Scotch-Irish Settlement in Virginia, Volume 2*, Kindle edition (The Commonwealth Printing Company: 1912), 397; Lyman Chalkley, *Chronicles of the Scotch-Irish Settlement in Virginia, Volume 1*, Kindle edition (The Commonwealth Printing Company: 1912), 3; Lyman Chalkley, *Chronicles of the Scotch-Irish Settlement in Virginia, Volume 2*, Kindle edition (The Commonwealth Printing Company: 1912), 397.

[16] Lyman Chalkley, *Chronicles of the Scotch-Irish Settlement in Virginia, Volume 1*, Kindle edition (The Commonwealth Printing Company: 1912), 475; Chalkley, *Chronicles of the Scotch-Irish Settlement in Virginia, Volume 2*, 3.

militias for protection, and Michael understood this.[17] Listed as a member of his local militia, it was his responsibility to defend his fellow settlers from Indian attacks.[18] One can imagine his sense of urgency, knowing that he was responsible for saving lives in case of an emergency. At their worst, *"The Indian raids were so fierce that whole families were being wiped out, or some killed and the rest taken captive"*, and *"Some of the frontier families gave up their homesteads and moved back to more populous areas"*.[19]

By August 1774, the animosity between Europeans and the Indians had reached a boiling point. The increasingly frequent raids by Native Americans on the Virginia frontier forced the Royal Governor, Lord Dunmore, to retaliate. Personally marching with his army into Ohio to confront the Indians, Lord Dunmore achieved victory at the Battle of Point Pleasant.[20] Afterwards, a peace treaty was signed with the Native Americans that prohibited them from raiding south of Ohio.

In July 1775, Michael Kelly is recorded as being compensated for 121 days of service under Captain George Matthew's company in Dunmore's War.[21] The events that he participated in must have been disturbing and gloomy, but yet also rewarding. Being a political refuge himself, Michael's experience was no different than the Native Americans. Both were political and religious victims of the English government, and they only desired a better life for themselves. Happy to have served and protected his fellow Scots-Irish from being taken captive, he also realized that the ancestral land of the Indians was slowly being taken away. This tragedy must have been evident when Captain George Matthew's company performed a maneuver that led to the defeat

---

[17] Robert P. Davis, James H. Smylie, Dean K. Thompson, Ernest Trice Thompson, William Newton Todd, *Virginia Presbyterians in American Life: Hanover Presbytery (1755-1980)* (Richmond, Virginia: Hanover Presbytery, 1982), 33.

[18] Larry J Hoefling, *Scots and Scotch Irish: Frontier Life in North Carolina,, Virginia, And Kentucky* (Oklahoma: Inlandia Press, 2009), 151.

[19] Davis, Symlie, Thompson, Thompson, Todd, *Virginia Presbyterians in AmericanLife: Hanover Presbytery (1755-1980)*, 33.

[20] Library of Virginia, *Library of Virginia* (http://www.lva.virginia.gov: accessed 28 December 2016), "About the Dunmore's War (Virginia Payrolls/Public Service Claims, 1775) Collection."

[21] Library of Virginia, "Virginia Payrolls/Public Service Claims, 1775," database with images, *Library of Virginia* (http://www.lva.virginia.gov: accessed 28 December 2016), entry for Michael Kelly, George Matthew's company.

of the Shawnee Indians.[22] The result of which led to the future loss of more Native American land.

With this bitter-sweet victory, Michael had completed another job to provide for his newly-wedded wife, Mary Thompson. On April 26, 1772, they were married in Bedford County, Virginia, where Mary's family was from.[23] Despite his unfortunate experiences, he was able to purchase 52 acres of land in Bedford County, Virginia, on March 22, 1773, and 15 acres of land in Bedford County on September 27, 1773.[24]

Over the years, Michael Kelly's social status had risen and by March 1774, he was earning money through more dignified means. One common methodology was to earn money by attending court as a paid witness. Allowed seven "*Dais*" or days in court, he put forth a motion that William James pay him for his attendance.[25] Within the same year, Michael is a security for William Farlin who was arrested for being in debt. William Farlin bail was paid, and it is probable that Michael was responsible for paying it.[26]

As timed passed, Michael Kelly and his family lived an ordinary life. Michael would return home from a hard day's work while Mary Thompson, like most women, tended to the children and the home. However, the Kelly family also had cheerful occasions as well. For Michael, the income he earned provided food and shelter for his newly-born son, Joseph. The only known child of Michael and Mary Kelly, Joseph was born abt. 1778. However, Michael soon became involved in the most important conflict of his time: the American Revolution.

---

[22] Author not listed, *Chapter 1: Clash at Point Pleasant*, 39-40; digital images, *Pelicanpub.com* (http://pelicanpub.com/content/9781589805033_CH1.pdf: accessed 28 December 2016).

[23] Rowland D. Buford, *Marriage Bonds of Bedford County, Virginia, 1755-1800* (Baltimore, Maryland: Genealogical Publishing Co., 38; Katherine Elizabeth Kelley, "*Kelley* [1972]," p. 21; The Bassett Historical Library, Bassett, Virginia.

[24] Bedford County, Virginia, Deed Book. No 5 (1773-1778): 27-28, Walton to Kelly; Microfilm 2; Library of Virginia, Richmond; Bedford County, Virginia, Deed Book. No 5 (1773-1778): 132-133, Helton to Kelly; Microfilm 2; Library of Virginia, Richmond.

[25] Bedford County, Virginia, Order Book. No 5-B (1774): 91, Michael Kelly; Microfilm 40; Library of Virginia, Richmond.

[26] Bedford County, Virginia, Order Book. No 6 (1774-1782): 202, George Buchanan vs Wm M. Farlin, Michael Kelly; Microfilm 40; Library of Virginia, Richmond.

Enlisting on September 20, 1777 in the 14th Virginia regiment as a continental solider, Michael Kelly experienced historic but dangerous circumstances.[27] Documented as being present at the New Brunswick encampment on July 6, 1778, Michael probably fought in the Battle of Monmouth on June 28, 1778.[28] Known as the last major battle of the war until the Battle of Yorktown, this conflict resulted in 360 American deaths and 358 British deaths.[29]

Disorganized and resulting in a retreat, Washington's army became demoralized. After watching the militia advance into a wall of bayonets, Michael Kelly saw a spooked General Charles Lee retreat.[30] However, a brave George Washington ordered his solders into formation and personally charged into battle. Neither side claimed victory, but Washington's act inspired the Continental Army, giving them hope for future battles.

Stationed at West Point, New Jersey, in September 1788, Michael Kelly did not experience any armed conflict, but rather a lack of supplies, inflation, and an approaching winter.[31] He also likely participated in the construction of the fortifications at the military encampment. Beginning in 1778, under the guidance of Chief Engineer Colonel Louis de la Radiere, Michael probably worked on building hospitals, docks, forges, barracks, storehouses, and even markets.[32] On September 15, 1778, General George Washington had his Quartermaster, Nathaniel Greene,

---

[27] Michael Kelley, Capt. Syrus L. Robert's Company, Virginia Muster Roll, 20 September 1777; 1st & 10th Virginia Regiment, 1779, box 9; Revolutionary War payrolls, 1776-1784; Library of Richmond, Virginia, microfilm.

[28] Michael Kelley, Capt. Syrus L. Robert's Company, Virginia Muster Roll, 6 July 1778, 1st & 10th Virginia Regiment, 1779, box 9; Revolutionary War payrolls, 1776-1784; Library of Richmond, Virginia, microfilm.

[29] Andrew Stough, *Sons of the American Revolution* (http://www.revolutionarywararchives.org/: 12 January 2017), "The American Revolution Month-by Month, June 1778."

[30] Stough, *Sons of the American Revolution*, "The American Revolution Month-by Month, June 1778."

[31] Andrew Stough, *Sons of the American Revolution* (http://www.revolutionarywararchives.org/: 12 January 2017), "The American Revolution Month-by Month, September 1778."

[32] Kris Brown and Matthew Fletcher, "*Historic Structures Report Logistical and Quartermaster Operations at Fortress West Point, 1778-1783,*"p. 5-7; digital images, *Hudsonrivervalley.org* (http://www.hudsonrivervalley.org/library/pdfs/articles_books_essays/westpointlogistics_c ubbison.pdf: accessed 11 February 2017).

direct the assembly of *"Magazines of forages for a winter stock,"* at West point. With Michael already living in the encampment, it is possible that he helped with this project.[33]

The importance of constructing these storehouses cannot be overrrstated. Necessary for survival, Michael's Kelly's effort in these construction projects provided supplies for the approaching winter. From October 1778 to December 24, 1778, Michael is stationed at the Middle Brook camp in New Jersey.[34] Recorded as being on furlough, he was not on active duty. It is unknown why he is on furlough; however, it is likely that he went home to visit his family and friends.

He is next recorded as being active in August 1779 when another historic battle took place, the Battle of Newton. American forces led by General John Sullivan and James Clinton were ambushed by an army of British loyalists and Native Americans.[35] Although the American colonists defeated their attackers, they destroyed the villages and supplies of the Indians afterwards in an act of retribution. Michael Kelly's location is not recorded; however, if he was present at the Battle of Newton, he would have had to fight against the Native Americans a second time, despite his opinion on the matter.

By November 1779, Michael was stationed at a camp near Morristown in New Jersey at a time when the focus of the war had shifted to the South.[36] *"Supposed to be with Gen Scott southwardly"* in the Southern Campaign, he instead experienced an *"unusually severe"* winter

---

[33] Kris Brown and Matthew Fletcher, *"Historic Structures Report Logistical and Quartermaster Operations at Fortress West Point, 1778-1783,"*p. 27; digital images, *Hudsonrivervalley.org*
(http://www.hudsonrivervalley.org/library/pdfs/articles_books_essays/westpointlogistics_c ubbison.pdf: accessed 11 February 2017).

[34] Michael Kelley, Capt. Syrus L. Robert's Company, Virginia Muster Roll, October 1778, 24 December 1778; 1st & 10th Virginia Regiment, 1779, box 9; Revolutionary War payrolls, 1776-1784; Library of Richmond, Virginia, microfilm.

[35] National Park Service, *National Park Service* (https://www.nps.gov/: accessed February 26, 2017), "Revolution Day by Day, August 29, 1779"; Michal Kelly, Captain John Overton's Company, Virginia Muster Roll, August – September 6, 1779; 1st & 10th Virginia Regiment, 1779, box 9; Revolutionary War payrolls, 1776-1784; Library of Richmond, Virginia, microfilm.

[36] Mical Kelly, Captain John Overton's Company, Virginia Muster Roll, November 1779; 1st & 10th Virginia Regiment,1779, box 9; Revolutionary War payrolls, 1776-1784; Library of Richmond, Virginia, microfilm.

where the Harbor of New York had frozen.[37] Sickness, poor morale, and death were a frequent problem for the Northern army. Food and clothing weren't readily available nor was there enough cash to buy local supplies.

The misery of that winter; however, was only a footnote in Michael's life. By February 20, 1780, he was living in Henry County, Virginia.[38] Having finished his 3 year term in the army, he is documented as providing money for the war effort. Inflation had become a problem due to the rising costs of imports. The British navy successfully blocked the ports of the coastal cities which raised the price of foreign products. The industries that exported tobacco, the crash crop of Virginia, were also hindered.

Three year later on September 1, 1783, two days before the end of the American Revolution, Michael Kelly buys 395 acres of land in neighboring Pittsylvania County, Virginia.[39] Now an established settler with financial support, a family, and friends, he could afford to purchase more land. With the memories of how he had to forfeit his right of 50 acres of land still fresh, he built a new life for himself and his family.

With land to grow corn and tobacco, Michael became a farmer. Gone were the days of soldiering and long days of travel. No Longer did he have to take on jobs that new immigrants accepted, nor did he have to continue to establish social networks. He now had the means to make a modest life as is evident on June 24, 1783, when he purchased 465 acres of land in Henry County.[40] This streak of prosperity

---

[37] Andrew Stough, *Sons of the American Revolution* (http://www.revolutionarywararchives.org/: accessed 25 February 2017), "The American Revolution Month-by Month, November 1779."

[38] Lela C. Adams, *1778-1780 Tax Lists of Henry County, Virginia* (Easley, Southern Carolina: Southern Historical Press. Inc., 1989), 27.

[39] "Online Catalog: Images & indexes," database with images, *The Library of Virginia* (http://lva1.hosted.exlibrisgroup.com: accessed 18 December 2016), Michael Kelly, 1 September 1783, Virginia, Colonial Land Office, Patents, 1623-1774; Library of Virginia.

[40] Henry County, Virginia, Deed Book. 2 (1780-1784): 340-341, Michael Kelly; Microfilm 1; Library of Virginia, Richmond.

continued into the following year when he bought 200 acres of land, also in Henry County.[41]

By September 9, 1793, Joseph Kelly, his son had probably reached adulthood, and Michael began to sell some of his land, beginning with fifty acres of land in Patrick County.[42] On Aug 30, 1794, he sold an additional, unnamed amount of land in Patrick County, Virginia.[43] Around this time, Michael Kelly disappears from the genealogical record, and therefore, it can be concluded that he probably died. Unfortunately, he did not get to see Joseph marry Jane Hill in 1815 in Patrick County.[44]

Children

The Children of Michael Kelly and Mary Thompson are as follows:

- JOSEPH KELLY, probably born in Bedford County, Virginia; died about 1815 in Patrick County, Virginia.[45] He married Jane Hill in 1815 in Patrick County.[46]

Conclusion

The struggle of the eighteenth-century Scots-Irish worker often involved hardship. Fresh off the boat, immigrants like Michael Kelly worked their way up in society. Taking jobs that only poor workers agreed to do, he eventually became involved in the American Revolution. Like numerous other Scots-Irish Immigrants, Michael also participated in the Northern Campaign from 1778-1779, and in Lord Dunmore's War in

---

[41] Henry County, Virginia, Deed Book. 2 (1780-1784): 112, Michael Kelly; Microfilm 1; Library of Virginia, Richmond.

[42] Patrick County, Virginia, Deed Book. 1 (1791-1801): 127, Michael Kelly, Microfilm 1; Library of Virginia, Richmond.

[43] Patrick County, Virginia, Deed Book. 1 (1791-1801): 231, Michael Kelley, Microfilm 1; Library of Virginia, Richmond.

[44] Patrick County, Virginia, Marriage Bonds (1815-1819), Joseph Kelly, 1815, recorded bond with license (with original signatures) and returns, Microfilm 54; Library of Virginia, Richmond.

[45] Patrick County, Virginia, Will Book No. 2 (1823- 1838): (), Inventory of Joseph Kelly, 1836, microfilm 14; Library of Virginia, Richmond.

[46] Patrick County, Virginia, Marriage Bonds (1815-1819), Joseph Kelly, 1815.

1774. The income earned from his military service provided him a stable, financial foundation to support his family and his modest lifestyle.

- Importing himself from Ireland in 1754, Michael is recorded in court in Orange County, Virginia, as forfeiting his right of fifty acres of land. This is probably because he could not support and maintain this land by himself.[47]

- In 1754, Michael is recorded *"for taking up a runaway negroman,"* in an attempt to establish social networks, to earn income, and to work his way up in society.[48]

- On August 10, 1754, Michael is requesting to be added to the tithable list of his local parish.[49]

- By 1755, Michael is recorded as working in husbandry in Augusta County, Virginia.[50] Six years later on February 18, 1761, he receives twenty-five lashes for *"taking a horse without a press warrant."*[51] One year later in May 1762, he is paid £1, 15 for driving cattle for 20 days.[52]

- Due to the frequent conflicts with Native Americans on the Virginia frontier, Michael joined the militia of Augusta County.[53] This provided him with income and a chance to protect his community.

- In Lord Dunmore's War in 1774, Michael served under George Matthew's Company. As part of the militia, this was Michael's first major military conflict.[54]

---

[47] Orange County, Virginia, Order Book. No 5: 36, microfilm 32.

[48] Orange County, Virginia, Order Book. No 6: 36, microfilm 32.

[49] Orange County, Virginia, Order Book. No 5: 37, microfilm 32.

[50] Lyman Chalkley, *Chronicles of the Scotch-Irish Settlement in Virginia, Volume 2*, 397.

[51] Lyman Chalkley, *Chronicles of the Scotch-Irish Settlement in Virginia, Volume 1*, 475.

[52] Lyman Chalkley, *Chronicles of the Scotch-Irish Settlement in Virginia, Volume 1*.

[53] Larry J Hoefling, *Scots and Scotch Irish: Frontier Life in North Carolina,, Virginia, And Kentucky*, 151; Davis, Symlie, Thompson, Thompson, Todd, *Virginia Presbyterians in American Life: Hanover Presbytery (1755-1980)*, 33.

[54] Library of Virginia, "Virginia Payrolls/Public Service Claims, 1775" entry for Michael Kelly, George Matthew's company.

20

- By September 27, 1773, Michael Kelly had purchased 67 acres of land in Bedford County, Virginia, despite his unfortunate start in the new world.[55]
- In March 1774, Michael put forth a motion that William James pay him for his attendance in court as a more dignified way to earn income.[56] That same year, he probably pays the bail for William Farlin in Bedford County.[57] This concludes that he had finally formed social networks.
- Enlisting on September 20, 1777 in the 14th Virginia regiment as a solider of the Continental Army, Michael served in the American Revolution until December 1779.[58]
- In 1780, Michael Kelly is recorded as providing revenue for the American Revolution in Henry County, Virginia. This is an indication that he surpassed his financial troubles.[59]
- By June 24, 1783, Michael had reached the height of his achievement after purchasing 465 acres of land in Henry County, Virginia. Additionally, on September 1, 1783, he bought 395 acres of land in Pittsylvania County, Virginia.[60]

[55] Bedford County, Virginia, Deed Book. No 5: 27-28, Microfilm 2; Bedford County, Virginia, Deed Book. No 5: 132-133, Microfilm 2.

[56] Bedford County, Virginia, Order Book. No 5-B: 91, Microfilm 40.

[57] Bedford County, Virginia, Order Book. No 6: 202, Microfilm 40.

[58] Michael Kelley, Capt. Syrus L. Robert's Company, Virginia Muster Roll, 20 September 1777, October 1778, 24 December 1778; 1st & 10th Virginia Regiment, 1779, box 9; Revolutionary War payrolls, 1776-1784; Library of Richmond, Virginia, microfilm; Michal Kelly, Captain John Overton's Company, Virginia Muster Roll, 20 September 1777, November-December 9; 1st & 10th Virginia Regiment,1779, box9.

[59] Lela C. Adams, *1778-1780 Tax Lists of Henry County, Virginia*, 27.

[60] "Online Catalog: Images & indexes," images, *The Library of Virginia*, Michael Kelly, 1 September 1783, Virginia, Colonial Land Office, Patents, 1623-1774; Henry County, Virginia, Deed Book. 2, 340-341.

Chapter 3
Nicholas Meriwether II

The English settlers of colonial Virginia became some of the most powerful and influential inhabitants in the area. With their early arrival in the colony, they passed down their wealth to their children who also rose into high society. Like other frontiersmen, they suffered the same hardships and experienced the same joyful occasions; however, these Englishmen had a political and economic advantage. Becoming merchants, large landowners, and politicians, they influenced the colony for better or worse.

Nicholas Meriwether II of Hanover County, Virginia, is among this group of wealthy settlers. The son of an English or Welsh immigrant, Nicholas became one of the largest landowners in Virginia from 1698 to his death in 1744.

Nicholas Meriwether Born about 1665 in Surry County, Virginia; died in 1744 in Albemarle County, Virginia.[1] He married Elizabeth Crawford.

Nicholas's Percentage

Born to Nicholas Meriwether I and Elizabeth, Nicholas Meriwether II was a first generation American. Nicholas Meriwether I immigrated from England or Wales before July 4, 1653 and became a *"Clerk of the Quarter Court and Governor's Council"*.[2] From July 4, 1653 when Nicholas Meriwether I brought 300 acres of land in Lancaster County, Virginia, to April 25, 1667, when he purchased 850 acres of land in Surry

---

[1] Nelson Heath Meriwether, *The Meriwether's and their Connections* (Columbia, Missouri: Artcraft Press, 1964), 1, 8, 9, 20, 21; The Meriwether Society, Inc., The Meriwether Society, Inc.: Family Groups: M12 Nicholas II (1665-1744) and Elizabeth (Crafford/Crawford) (http://tmsi.j777.org/: accessed 20 October 2016).

[2] The Meriwether Society, Inc., *The Meriwether Society, Inc.: Family Groups: M1 Nicholas I (1631-1678) and Elizabeth (unknown)* (http://tmsi.j777.org/: accessed 20 October 2016), "Nicholas served as a clerk of the Quarter Court and Governor's Council."

County, Virginia, Nicholas had purchased a total of 2,977 acres of land.[3] Nicholas Meriwether II's childhood and future adult life was influenced by his father's political and economic endeavors, so much so, that he surpassed his father's achievements.

Life Story

Nicholas Meriwether II was raised in a family whose values centered on the cultural elite of James City, the capital of Virginia. Nicholas Meriwether I's career impressed upon Nicholas Meriwether II the importance of adopting this way of life. As a child, Nicholas knew of and heard stories about his father's experience as a member of the Governor's Council.[4] He also knew about the economic and political advantages associated with it.

As the son of a prominent politician, Nicholas Meriwether II lived a privileged life in a society of inequality. Born in Surry County, Virginia, which broke off from James City in 1652, Nicholas's family had acquired a vast wealth.[5] Unlike other planters who weren't large landowners, Nicholas was destined to help shape the history of central Virginia.

One can imagine the sense of responsibility that Nicholas must have felt, knowing he was expected to be a leader. With Nicholas Meriwether I being active in the colonial government, Nicholas Meriwether II learned that the upper class influenced the colony economically and politically. As a result, he understood the importance of expanding the frontier by buying vast amounts of land. Nicholas

---

[3] "Online Catalog: Images & indexes," database with images, *The Library of Virginia* (http://lva1.hosted.exlibrisgroup.com: accessed 29 October 2016), Nicholas Meriwether, 4 July 1653, 16 November 1653, 15 December 1656, 23 October 1656, 6 November 1661, 25 April 1667, 25 April 1667, Virginia, Colonial Land Office, Patents, 1623-1774; Library of Virginia.

[4] The Meriwether Society, Inc., *The Meriwether Society, Inc.: Family Groups: M1 Nicholas I (1631-1678) and Elizabeth (unknown)*, "Nicholas served as a clerk of the Quarter Court and Governor's Council."

[5] Nelson Heath Meriwether, *The Meriwether's and their Connections*, "1, 8, 9, 20,21.";
Iberian Publishing Company, *Iberian Publish Company's On-Line Catalog: The Growth of Virginia, 1634-1895, 1651-1660* (http://genealogyresources.org/Va_map_1650.html: accessed 11 December 2016), "1652 - Surry (James City)."

Meriwether I himself had purchased a total of 2,977 acres of land to grow Tobacco, Virginia's crash crop.[6]

In 1668 Nicholas Meriwether II is living in New Kent County, Virginia, on the frontier. At 24 years of age, Nicholas has not yet purchased the large tracts of land that his father had acquired; however, he had started his political career. On March 19, 1668, Nicholas is appointed a vestryman and becomes an official in the colonial government.[7] His duties allowed him to move up in society for greater access to land grants. Eventually, he became one of the largest and most influential landowners in central Virginia.

As a member of the upper class, Nicholas lived a multipurpose life. While farmers tilled the fields, grew crops, and lived ordinary lives, statesmen held positions of power. Privy to the decision making progress for St. Peter's Parish, Nicholas formed the backbone of the local parish.[8] Because church and state were one entity in Virginia, he collected levies for the English government.[9] His responsibility to expand the frontier was also directly linked to his wealth.

Land was an important form of wealth in the eighteenth-century and those who strategically purchased land on the frontier could make a profit from it.[10] By April 6, 1702, Nicholas Meriwether II was appointed a churchwarden, moving him closer to his goal of becoming an influential landowner.[11] In charge of "*making of presentments for trial on*

---

[6] "Online Catalog: Images & indexes," images, *The Library of Virginia*, Nicholas Meriwether, 4 July 1653, 16 November 1653, 15 December 1656, 23 October 1656,6 November 1661, 25 April 1667, 25 April 1667, Virginia, Colonial Land Office, Patents, 1623-1774.

[7] St. Peter's Parish, *The Vestry Book of Saint Peter's: New Kent County, Va. from 1682-1758* (Scholar's Choice, 2015), 49-50.

[8] St. Peter's Parish, *The Vestry Book of Saint Peter's: New Kent County, Va. from 1682-1758*, 49-50.

[9] St. Peter's Parish, *The Vestry Book of Saint Peter's: New Kent County, Va. from 1682-1758* (Scholar's Choice, 2015), 55-56; St. Peter's Parish, *The Vestry Book of Saint Peter's: New Kent County, Va. from 1682-1758* (Scholar's Choice, 2015), 71-72.

[10] Wesley Frank Craven, *The Colonies in the Seventeenth Century, 1607-1689* (LSU Press, 2015), 181; digital images, Google Books (http://www.books.google.com: accessed 16 December 2016).

[11] St. Peter's Parish, *The Vestry Book of Saint Peter's: New Kent County, Va. from 1682-1758* (Scholar's Choice, 2015), 64-66.

complaints of drunkenness, swearing, sabbathbreaking, recusancy, fornication, adultery, bastardy, and other such offences", he became associated with those in power.[12] By April 20, 1704, when St. Paul's Parish was established in New Kent County, Nicholas was again elected a Vestryman.[13]

As a Vestryman of St. Peter's Parish, only the *"most able and discreet persons of their parish"* were chosen to represent the Church of England.[14]

Over the years, Nicholas Meriwether's prestige grew until he became one of the first members of the House of Burgesses for Hanover County, Virginia, in 1712.[15] As part of the *"first democratically-elected legislative body"* in the new world, Nicholas had reached the height of his career.[16]

Officially part of the highest ranks of society, he had greater responsibilities. The roles he performed in the House of Burgesses; although, politically stressful, granted him access to highly prized land grants. Serving from 1712 to 1714, 1720 to 1722, and then from 1723 to 1734, his duties consisted of being a member of the General Assembly, a member of the Committee for Propositions and Grievances, and a member of the Committee of Elections for Privileges.[17]

---

[12] Wesley Frank Craven, *The Colonies in the Seventeenth Century, 1607-1689*, 181.

[13] Virginia State Library and Archives, *The Vestry Book of St. Paul's Parish: Hanover County, Virginia (1706-1786)* (1940; reprint, Richmond, Virginia: Virginia State Library and Archives, 1989), 594.

[14] Virginia State Library and Archives, *The Vestry Book of St. Paul's Parish: Hanover County, Virginia (1706-1786)*, 594.

[15] Library Board, Virginia State Library, *Journals of the House of Burgesses of Virginia, 1712-1714, 1715, 1718, 1720-1722, 1723-1726* (Richmond, Virginia: The Colonial Press, E. Waddey Co., 1905), 12; digital images, *Google Books* (http://www.books.google.com: accessed: 16 October 2016); Online Catalog: Images & indexes," database with images, *The Library of Virginia* (http://lva1.hosted.exlibrisgroup.com: accessed 29 October 2016), Nicholas Meriwether, 16 June 1714, Virginia, Colonial Land Office, Patents, 1623-1774; Library of Virginia.

[16] Maria Kimberly, *George Washington's Mount Vernon* (http://www.mountvernon.org/digital-encyclopedia/article/house-of-burgesses/: accessed 20 January 2017), "House of Burgesses."

[17] Library Board, Virginia State Library, *Journals of the House of Burgesses of Virginia, 1712-1714, 1715, 1718, 1720-1722, 1723-1726* (Richmond, Virginia: The Colonial Press, E. Waddey Co., 1905), 12; digital images, *Archive.org* (https://archive.org/: accessed: 16 October 2016); Library Board, Virginia State Library, *Journals of the House of Burgesses of Virginia, 1712-1714, 1715, 1718, 1720-1722, 1723-1726* (Richmond, Virginia: The Colonial Press, E. Waddey Co., 1905), 15; digital images, *Archive.org* (https://archive.org/:

Nicholas's contribution to the House of Burgesses proved to be of significance to the English Government. A bill sponsored by Nicholas Meriwether on March 27, 1728 that "*Intituled an Act for better fecuring the paiment of Levies and Reftraint of vagrants & idle people, And for the effectual discovery & perfecution of pefons having Baftard Children,*" was passed to support the Church of England.[18] A controversial act, it allowed the colonial government to secure church tithes with more authority, punish those who did not pay, and persecute infidelity with less restrictions.

He also participated in sessions where the rights of Native Americans were discussed. Although, his name is not recorded, he probably voted for a bill that provided, "*proper methods [to erect] and [to maintain] schools in order to the training of Youths to reading and to a neceffary knowledge of the Principles of Religion and to encourage the Converfion of Negros and Indians to the Chriftian Religion.*"[19]

Because of the unity between church and state, the House of Burgesses debated issues that were both secular and ecclesiastical. As a result, Nicholas Meriwether II's service to the Church of England was well rewarded. By 1737, Nicholas had purchased a total of 49,584 acres of land from several counties. In New Kent County, he purchased 8,340 areas[20], 39, 604 acres in Hanover County[21], and 1,640 acres in Goochland

---

accessed: 16 October 2016); Library Board, Virginia State Library, *Journals of the House of Burgesses of Virginia, 1727-1734, 1736-1740* (Richmond, Virginia: The Colonial Press, E. Waddey Co., 1905), 10; digital images, *Archive.org* (https://archive.org/: accessed: 16 October 2016); Library Board, Virginia State Library, *Journals of the House of Burgesses of Virginia, 1712-1714, 1715, 1718, 1720-1722, 1723-1726* (Richmond, Virginia: The Colonial Press, E. Waddey Co., 1905), 14; digital images, *Archive.org* (https://archive.org/: accessed: 16 October 2016); Virginia, General Assembly, House of Burgesses, *Journals of the House of Burgesses of Virginia* (Richmond, Virginia: Library Board, Virginia State Library, 1619), 78, 322; digital images, *Archive.org* (https://archive.org/: accessed January 20 2017).

[18] Virginia, General Assembly, House of Burgesses, *Journals of the House of Burgesses of Virginia* (Richmond, Virginia: Library Board, Virginia State Library, 1619), 46, ; digital images, *Archive.org* (https://archive.org/: accessed February 2 2017).

[19] Virginia, General Assembly, House of Burgesses, *Journals of the House of Burgesses of Virginia* (Richmond, Virginia: Library Board, Virginia State Library, 1619), 63, ; digital images, *Archive.org* (https://archive.org/: accessed February 2 2017).

[20] "Online Catalog: Images & indexes," database with images, *The Library of Virginia* (http://lva1.hosted.exlibrisgroup.com: accessed 2 February 2017), Nicholas Meriwether, 16 June 1714, Virginia, Colonial Land Office, Patents, 1623-1774; Library of Virginia.

[21] "Online Catalog: Images & indexes," database with images, *The Library of Virginia* (http://lva1.hosted.exlibrisgroup.com: accessed 2 February 2017), Nicholas Meriwether, 18 February 1722, 5 September 1723, 31 October 1726, 31 October 1726, 31 October 1726, 16

County.[22] By owning a vast amount of land, Nicholas could certainly support himself and his family with tobacco.

Nicholas Meriwether and Elizabeth Crawford had a total of 7 children with 3 sons and 4 daughters. Around 1744, Nicholas passed away in Goochland County, Virginia, and recorded the names of his children in his will. William, David, and Nicholas were included among his sons, and Ann, Elizabeth, Sarah, and Jane were recorded as his daughters.[23] By this time, his children had married into other affluent families as well.

Children

The Children of Nicholas Meriwether II and Elizabeth Crawford are as follows:

- WILLIAM MERIWETHER, born in James City County, Virginia; died before October 15, 1751.[24] He married Elizabeth Bushrod about 1712.[25]
- DAVID MERIWETHER, born in James City County or New Kent County abt. 1680; died December 25, 1744 in Louisa

June 1727, 27 September 1729, 27 September 1729, 9 July 1730, 28 September 1730, 28 September 1730, 29 September 1733, 15 March 1735, Virginia, Colonial Land Office, Patents, 1623-1774; Library of Virginia.

[22] "Online Catalog: Images & indexes," database with images, *The Library of Virginia* (http://lva1.hosted.exlibrisgroup.com: accessed 2 February 2017), Nicholas Meriwether, 10 June 1737, 19 July 1735, 21 November 1734, Virginia, Colonial Land Office, Patents, 1623-1774; Library of Virginia.

[23] Goochland County, Virginia, "Goochland County, Virginia, Deed Book No. 4 (1741-1745),"p. 437-443, Nicholas Meriwether will, 12 December 1743; Library of Virginia, Microfilm 2; The National Society of the Colonial Dames of America in the State of Virginia, *The Parish Register of Saint Peter's Parish, New Kent County, Virginia from 1680-1787* (1988; reprint, Richmond, Virginia: Wm Ellis Jones, Book and Job Printer, 1904), 23-24.

[24] Virginia State Library and Archives, *The Vestry Book of St. Paul's Parish: Hanover County, Virginia (1706-1786)* (1940; reprint, Richmond, Virginia: Virginia State Library and Archives, 1989),327- 329; The Meriwether Society, Inc., *The Meriwether Society, Inc.: Family Groups: M1 Nicholas I (1631-1678) and Elizabeth Crawford* (http://tmsi.j777.org/: accessed 3 February 2017), "William Meriwether."; Goochland County, Virginia, "Goochland County, Virginia, Deed Book No. 4 (1741-1745),"p. 437-443.

[25] The Meriwether Society, Inc., *The Meriwether Society, Inc.,* "William Meriwether."

County, Virginia.[26] He married Anne Holmes around 1713 in New Kent County, Virginia.[27]

- NICHOLAS MERIWETHER III, born July 11, 1699 in New Kent County, Virginia; died after Jun 5, 1714.[28]

- ANN JOHNSON MERIWETHER, born July 15, 169[?] in New Kent County, Virginia; died March 1785 in Louisa County, Virginia.[29] She married Thomas Johnson around 1712.[30]

- ELIZABETH BRAY MERIWETHER, born June 20, 1703 in New Kent County; died January 4, 1723/4.[31] She married Thomas Bray around 1724.[32]

- SARAH LITTLEPAGE MERIWETHER, born 1697; died July 2, 1733.[33] She married William Littlepage abt.1718.[34]

---

[26] The Meriwether Society, Inc., *The Meriwether Society, Inc.: Family Groups: M1 Nicholas I (1631-1678) and Elizabeth Crawford* (http://tmsi.j777.org/: accessed 3 February 2017), "Col. David Meriwether."; Virginia State Library and Archives, *The Vestry Book of St. Paul's Parish: Hanover County, Virginia (1706-1786)* (1940; reprint, Richmond, Virginia: Virginia State Library and Archives, 1989),307; Virginia Genealogical Society, *Louisa County [Virginia] Road Orders (1742-1748)* (1979; reprint, Westminster, Maryland: Heritage Books, Inc, 2008), 10,11; Goochland County, Virginia, "Goochland County, Virginia, Deed Book No. 4 (1741-1745),"p. 438, Nicholas Meriwether will, 12 December 1743; Library of Virginia, Microfilm 2.

[27] The Meriwether Society, Inc., *The Meriwether Society, Inc.,* "David Meriwether."

[28] The National Society of the Colonial Dames of America in the State of Virginia, *The Parish Register of Saint Peter's Parish, New Kent County, Virginia from 1680-1787* (1988; reprint, Richmond, Virginia: Wm Ellis Jones, Book and Job Printer, 1904), 23; The Meriwether Society, Inc., *The Meriwether Society, Inc.: Family Groups: M1 Nicholas I (1631-1678) and Elizabeth Crawford* (http://tmsi.j777.org/: accessed 3 February 2017), "Nicholas Meriwether III.

[29] Goochland County, Virginia, "Goochland County, Virginia, Deed Book No. 4, p. 438; The Meriwether Society, Inc., *The Meriwether Society, Inc.: Family Groups: M1 Nicholas I (1631-1678) and Elizabeth Crawford* (http://tmsi.j777.org/: accessed 3 February 2017), "Anne Meriwether."

[30] The Meriwether Society, Inc., *The Meriwether Society, Inc,* "Anne Meriwether."

[31] The National Society of the Colonial Dames of America in the State of Virginia, *The Parish Register of Saint Peter's Parish, New Kent County, Virginia from 1680-1787* (1988; reprint, Richmond, Virginia: Wm Ellis Jones, Book and Job Printer, 1904), 24; The Meriwether Society, Inc., *The Meriwether Society, Inc.: Family Groups: M1 Nicholas I (1631-1678) and Elizabeth Crawford* (http://tmsi.j777.org/: accessed 3 February 2017), "Elizabeth Meriwether."

[32] The Meriwether Society, Inc., *The Meriwether Society, Inc,* "Elizabeth Meriwether."

[33] The Meriwether Society, Inc., *The Meriwether Society, Inc.: Family Groups: M1 Nicholas I (1631-1678) and Elizabeth Crawford* (http://tmsi.j777.org/: accessed 3 February 2017), "Sarah Meriwether."

[34] The Meriwether Society, Inc., *The Meriwether Society, Inc,* "Sarah Meriwether.";
Goochland County, Virginia, "Goochland County, Virginia, Deed Book No. 4, p.438.

- JANE MERIWETHER, born abt. 1705; died before September 1757.[35] She married Colonel Robert Lewis abt. 1725.

Conclusion

The Genealogical narrative of Nicholas Meriwether II, although typical of an eighteenth-century gentlemen, is also atypical in several ways. All wealthy settlers in colonial Virginia owned more land than the average pioneer; however, because of Nicholas's large land holdings, he became an influential politician. Rising through the ranks from his local parish to the highest office in the colonial government, the House of Burgesses, he became a person of historic importance.

The son of Nicholas Meriwether I, a prominent immigrant, Nicholas Meriwether II grew accustomed to the life of a gentleman. His father's role as a Clerk for the Governor Council and for the Quarter Court inspired Nicholas Meriwether II to also become a man of influence.[36]

- On March 19, 1668, Nicholas Meriwether II is appointed to the position of vestryman in St. Peter's Parish in New Kent County, Virginia.[37] Officially beginning his political career, he participated in and voted on issues related to both Church and State.[38] Some of the issues involved *"drunkenness, swearing, sabbathbreaking, recusancy, fornication, adultery, bastardy, and other such offences."*[39]
- On April 20, 1704, Nicholas was appointed as Vestryman in St. Paul's Parish in New Kent County Virginia, and later

[35] Goochland County, Virginia, "Goochland County, Virginia, Deed Book No. 4 (1741-1745),"p. 439, Nicholas Meriwether will, 12 December 1743; Library of Virginia, Microfilm 2; The Meriwether Society, Inc., *The Meriwether Society, Inc.: Family Groups: M1 Nicholas I (1631-1678) and Elizabeth Crawford* (http://tmsi.j777.org/: accessed 3 February 2017), "Jane Meriwether."

[36] The Meriwether Society, Inc., *The Meriwether Society, Inc.*, Nicholas served as a clerk of the Quarter Court and Governor's Council.

[37] St. Peter's Parish, *The Vestry Book of Saint Peter's: New Kent County, Va. from 1682-1758*, 49-50.

[38] St. Peter's Parish, *The Vestry Book of Saint Peter's: New Kent County, Va. from 1682-1758* (Scholar's Choice, 2015), 55-56, 71-72.

[39] Wesley Frank Craven, *The Colonies in the Seventeenth Century, 1607-1689*, 181.

in Hanover County, Virginia, where only the "*most able and discreet persons of their parish*" were able to be elected.[40]

- Beginning in 1712, he became a member of the House of Burgesses, the first democratically-elected body in the new world. After his first term ended in 1714, he was reelected from 1720 to 1722, and then from 1723 to 1734. His main responsibilities were serving on the General Assembly, the Committee for Propositions and Grievances, and the Committee for Elections and Privileges.[41]

- On March 27, 1728, he supported a controversial bill that "*Intituled an Act for better fecuring the paiment of Levies and Reftraint of vagrants & idle people, And for the effectual discovery & perfection of pefons having Baftard Children.*"[42]

- Rewarded for his service to the English government, Nicholas Meriwether II received highly-valuable land grants that totaled up to 49,584 acres of land. By 1737, he had received 8,340 areas of land in New Kent County, Virginia[43], 39, 604 acres of land in Hanover County, Virginia[44], and 1,640 acres of land in Goochland County, Virginia.[45]

---

[40] Virginia State Library and Archives, *The Vestry Book of St. Paul's Parish: Hanover County, Virginia*, 594.

[41] Library Board, Virginia State Library, *Journals of the House of Burgesses of Virginia, 1712-1714, 1715, 1718, 1720-1722, 1723-1726*, 12, 15, 10, 14.

[42] Virginia, General Assembly, House of Burgesses, *Journals of the House of Burgesses of Virginia*, 46.

[43] "Online Catalog: Images & indexes," images, *The Library of Virginia*, Nicholas Meriwether, 16 June 1714, Virginia, Colonial Land Office, Patents, 1623-1774.

[44] "Online Catalog: Images & indexes," images, *The Library of Virginia*, Nicholas Meriwether, 18 February 1722, 5 September 1723, 31 October 1726, 31 October 1726, 31 October 1726, 16 June 1727, 27 September 1729, 27 September 1729, 9 July 1730, 28 September 1730, 28 September 1730, 29 September 1733, 15 March 1735, Virginia, Colonial Land Office, Patents, 1623-1774.

[45] "Online Catalog: Images & indexes," images, *The Library of Virginia*, Nicholas Meriwether, 10 June 1737, 19 July 1735, 21 November 1734, Virginia, Colonial Land Office, Patents, 1623-1774.

Chapter 4
Queen of the Pamunkey

The history of Native Americans in colonial Virginia is full of exploration, conflict, and exploitation. As colonists from the British Isles who migrated to the new world became influential, the Native Americans viewed the foreigners with caution. However, as relationships with the Europeans began to form, it was obvious who held the military and political power.

One important footnote in this history is the story of Cockacoeske, also known as the Queen of the Pamunkey.[1] A fierce advocate of the Pamunkey tribe, she lived in a world where her people were used by the English government for political and economic purposes. Ironically, she also had conflicts within the Native American community. Related to Powhatan, the Indian chief of the coastal plains of Virginia in 1607,[2] the tribes he once ruled had rejected the rule of the Pamunkey tribe. However, thanks to Cockacoeske's political cunning, she was able to regain this authority as well as improve Anglo-Indian relations

Cockacoeske: Born before 1656 in Virginia; died about July 1, 1686.[3] She had a relationship with an English planter named Capt. John West.[4]

---

[1] Library of Virginia, *Document 5, Native American Folder* (Richmond, Virginia: Library of Virginia), 7; Liz Sonneborn, *Chronology of American Indian History, Updated* Edition (New York, New York: Infobase Publishing, 2007), 71.

[2] Gregory A. Waselkov, Peter H. Wood, Thomas Hatley, *Powhatan's Mantle: Indians in the Colonial Southeast* (Nebraska: University of Nebraska, 2006),243, *Google Books* (http://www.google.books.com accessed 29 July 2017).

[3] Gregory A. Waselkov, Peter H. Wood, Thomas Hatley, *Powhatan's Mantle: Indians in the Colonial Southeast* (Nebraska: University of Nebraska, 2006),259, *Google Books* (http://www.google.books.com accessed 29 July 2017).

[4] Library of Virginia, *Document 5, Native American Folder*, 7; Library of Virginia, *Document 1, Native American Folder* (Richmond, Virginia: Library of Virginia), 1.

Cockacoeske's Parentage: Related to Opechancanough, the Pamunkey Chief responsible for the March 22, 1622 massacre of Jamestown,[5] she inherited the Pamunkey Chiefdom in 1656.[6]

Life Story: Raised in a culture hostile toward English settlers, Cockaocoeske, despite her past experiences, would become an advocate for Native American rights and an ally to the English. Growing up in the reign of Opechancanough,, chief of the Pamunkey Indians, she saw the decline of her tribe. The conflicts between the settlers of Jamestown and the Native Americans were unfortunate; however, Cockacoeske, would learn from these mistakes to become Queen of the Pamunkey.

A witness to the decline of the fur trade between the English settlers and the Indians, her people were eventually prohibited from walking freely in the British settlements. In truth, the cultural differences between the two parties could not be more different. Cockacoeske's land had slowly been taken away and was being used to plant tobacco. Being pushed further inland, the European ideology of owning land also clashed with Native American culture.

In her childhood, the English authorities were instructed *"To use means to convert"* the Indians into Christians.[7] Sir Francis Wyatt, the Royal Governor of Jamestown, received instructions from the King of England to do this by *"[conversing] with some ; each town to teach some children for the college intended to be built:"*[8] He was also told *"not to injure the natives;"*[9] however, from the viewpoint of Cockacoeske, she saw how misguided these polices were.

The following year, after a large, multi-pronged attack on Jamestown, the Second Anglo-Powhatan War had begun. Although, the attack on Jamestown on March 22, 1622 was designed to weaken and isolate the English, it was viewed by the colonists as an attempt to *"destroy"* them.[10]

---

[5] Susan Myra Kingsbury, *The Records of the Virginia Company of London* (Washington, D.C.: Government Printing Press, 1906), 550.

[6] Liz Sonneborn, *Chronology of American Indian History, Updated Edition*, 71.

[7] William Waller Hening, *The Statues at Large: Volume 1* (London, England: Forgotten Books, 2015), 114.

[8] William Waller Hening, *The Statues at Large: Volume 1*, 114.

[9] William Waller Hening, *The Statues at Large: Volume 1*, 114.

[10] James Douglas Rice, *Encyclopedia Virginia* (https://www.encyclopediavirginia.org: July 30, 2017), "Second Anglo-Powhatan War (1622-1632)."

As a result, a military campaign followed that weakened the Native American tribes.

Cockacoeske, by this time, heard how the English retreated to Jamestown. Satisfied by their victory, little did the Indians know the plan of retaliation the colonists would implement. The prolonged abandonment of the western English settlements was an illusion meant to trick the Pamunkey. Outnumbered, the colonists had to strike at the most venerable aspect of Native American society, their cornfields.

Pretending to concede, the English began by forging alliances with distant Indian chiefdoms. They also were waiting for the corn of the Native Americans to fully ripen before beginning the most crippling phase. Once the corn was harvestable, the colonists raided Indian villages to, "*Cutt downe*" and steal the corn.[11] With superior technology, such as guns and metal armor, this strategy continued even after the turning point of the war in 1624.

Now a young woman, the loss of their food supply concerned Cockacoeske as more tribes sought their independence from Opechancanough's alliance. This political setback led to a peace treaty in 1632. However, the documentation for this peace is now lost.

The troubles for Cockacoeske and her people; however, did not end there. The English economy improved due to the acquisition of Native American lands and to the harvesting of tobacco on the said land. Being pushed westward, Opechancanough planned another major raid on English lands in 1644,[12] starting the Third Anglo-Powhatan War. Instead of fully pursuing the English, the Pamunkey Chief's warriors again withdrew. The reason for this is not known; however, in comparison to the Second Anglo-Powhatan War, Opechancanough had a fewer number of tribes supporting him.[13]

---

[11] Susan Myra Kingsbury, ed., *The Records of the Virginia Company of London* (Washington, D.C.: United States Government Printing Office, 1933), 507.

[12] Gregory A. Waselkov, Peter H. Wood, Thomas Hatley, *Powhatan's Mantle: Indians in the Colonial Southeast* (Nebraska: University of Nebraska, 2006),244, *Google Books* (http://www.google.books.com accessed 31 July 2017).

[13] Helen C. Rountree, *Encyclopedia Virginia* (https://www.encyclopediavirginia.org: July 31, 2017), "Opechancanough (d (1646)."

Two years later in 1646, Cockacoeske learned about Opechancanough's death in a Jamestown prison.[14] Her experiences from the Anglo-Powhatan Wars were tragic events that forever shaped her world view. Due to the documentation on her from English sources, she was a skilled politician, and it is likely that she learned from the mistakes of Opechancanough. The troubles for the Pamunkey tribe; unfortunately, were only beginning.

In October 1646, Necotowance, the next in line for the Pamunkey chiefdom, agreed to pursue a peace treaty.[15] By now the demoralized Native Americans realized how dim their situation was and were forced to accept unfavorable terms. Foremost, Chief Necotowance had to *"acknowledge to hold his kingdome from the King's Ma'tie of England, and his successors be appointed or confirmed by the King's Governours from time to time"*[16]. This decision striped Virginia Indians of their independence for years to come.

As a tributary tribe under the King of England, the Pamunkey Indians were protected by the English Government in exchange for *"twenty beaver skins att the goeing away of Geese yearely."*[17]

The Treaty of Peace with Necotowance forever changed Anglo-Indian relations at the expense of Native Americans. As a result, Cockacoeske learned to be politically and socially cunning to succeed.

In addition to the aforementioned penalties imposed on them, the Pamunkey had to restrict their hunt to their own land upon *"paine of death"*, and were restricted to constructing a home on their own land. They even were assigned self-Identifying badges.[18]

---

[14] Gregory A. Waselkov, Peter H. Wood, Thomas Hatley, *Powhatan's Mantle: Indians in the Colonial Southeast* (Nebraska: University of Nebraska, 2006), 245, *Google Books* (http://www.google.books.com accessed 31 July 2017).

[15] William Waller Hening, *The Statues at Large: Volume 1* (London, England: Forgotten Books, 2015), 325.

[16] William Waller Hening, *The Statues at Large: Volume 1* (London, England: Forgotten Books, 2015), 326.

[17] William Waller Hening, *The Statues at Large: Volume 1*, 326.

[18] William Waller Hening, *The Statues at Large: Volume 1* (London, England: Forgotten Books, 2015), 324, 325.

By this time, the Indian alliance had collapsed. Unlike the previous generations of Native Americans, a new kind of Anglo-Powhatan relationship was developing, and Cockacoeske became a key figure in it. As news spread about the death of Totopotomoy in 1656, who inherited the chiefdom after Necotowance,[19] her time to rule was near.

Knowing that she would become the next Chief of the Pamunkey, Cockacoeske also realized the challenges that lay ahead. The Native American population had decreased due to disease, war, and the inability to expand their lands. While they were being restricted from moving near English Plantations to the east, to the west more powerful tribes were already established. Due to these troubles, their dependency on the English government became a common theme.

From the beginning, she realized she had to employ effective but subtle political policies. Being a weaker nation than the colony of Virginia, the Pamunkey Indians cooperated with the settlers despite their past grievances. This complicated relationship required her to take on roles that previous Chiefs would have frowned upon.

The initial years of her reign are largely undocumented; however, around this time she had a relationship with an English planter: Colonel John West. The nature of this relationship is unknown, but they had a son named Captain John West.[20] Breaking away from the traditions of her tribe, she married an outsider. If she could more closely align herself with the English, she could better serve her people.

Appearing before a committee of Indian affairs in Jamestown with her son in 1676, the Queen of the Pamunkey's allegiance with the English Crown was tested. Upon her arrival, she was asked how many Indians she could

---

[19] Gregory A. Waselkov, Peter H. Wood, Thomas Hatley, *Powhatan's Mantle: Indians in the Colonial Southeast* (Nebraska: University of Nebraska, 2006),245, *Google Books* (http://www.google.books.com accessed 31 July 2017).

[20] Library of Virginia, *Document 5, Native American Folder*, 7; Charles McLeanAndrews, *Narratives of the Insurrections, 1675-1690* (New York, New York: Charles Scribner's Sons, 1915), 25, Google books (Books.google.com: accessed 1 August 2017).

provide to help confront another Indian tribe, the Susquchannocks.[21] Distraught over the death of her husband, the previous King of the Pamunkey, she refused to answer and let her interpreter answer instead: "*Tatapamoi dead.*"[22] It was further explained that Totopotomoy died fighting for the English with no compensation offered. Dispassionately, the chairman pressed two more times, "*What Indians will you now Contribute?*"[23] Answering "*Twelve*" she angrily turned her back and walked out of the room.

This complicated, lukewarm relationship likely remained the same throughout her chiefdom. After years of warfare with the English colonists, the time for common ground was just beginning. Unfortunately, more often than not, it was pushed aside due to new conflicts. One of those, which devastated the Pamunkey Tribe and its allies, was their involvement in Bacon's Rebellion in 1676.

Nathaniel Bacon's rebellion against the next Royal Governor of Virginia, William Berkeley, was a menacing act that led to a new state of Indian affairs. The nature of this conflict was a power struggle between Nathaniel Bacon and William Berkeley. As an enemy of the English Government, Nathaniel commenced a surprise attack on the tributary Indians. As Cockcaoeske and her allies fled from the approaching mob, the rebels were "*killing and taking them prisoners.*" She watched in horror as "*Indian matts, basketts, matchcotes, parcels of wampampeag and Roanoke (w'ch is their money) in Baggs, Furrs, Pieces of Lynnen, Broad cloth, and divers sorts of English goods,*"[24] were taken.

The aftermath of this assault led to a rebirth of the Pamunkey alliance. In 1677, Cockacoeske and several other tribes signed the Treaty at Middle Plantation. Her decision to have a son with an Englishman, and the frustration she expressed towards the committee on Indian affairs

---

[21] Charles McLean Andrews, *Narratives of the Insurrections, 1675-1690* (New York, New York: Charles Scribner's Sons, 1915), 26, Google books (Books.google.com: accessed 2 August 2017).

[22] Charles McLean Andrews, *Narratives of the Insurrections, 1675-1690*, 26.

[23] Charles McLean Andrews, *Narratives of the Insurrections, 1675-1690* (New York, New York: Charles Scribner's Sons, 1915), 27, Google books (Books.google.com: accessed 2 August 2017).

[24] Charles McLean Andrews, *Narratives of the Insurrections, 1675-1690* (New York, New York: Charles Scribner's Sons, 1915), 127, Google books (Books.google.com: accessed 2 August 2017).

were part of a larger plan. If she could balance her tribe's needs and build a constructive relationship with the English, much could be accomplished.

Like the Peace treaty of October 1646, the agreement signed at Middle Plantation stated that all tributary Indians had *"to have their immediate Dependency on, and own all Subjection to the Great King of England, our Dread Sovereign, His Heirs and Successors, when they pay their Tributes to His Majesties Governour for the time being."*[25] It also declared that, *"the said Indian Kings and Queens and their Subjects, shall hold their Land,"* without any penalties.[26]

Written with more consideraten, this treaty gave the Queen of the Pamunkey the authority over all other, *"Indian King and Queen."*[27] Still unpopular with some of these tribes, Cockacoeske inherited a contentious and politically-charged situation. Although, the peace with the English settlers was now established, this compromise was not perfect.

Receiving a crown inscribed with *"The Queene of the Pamunkey,"* she achieved what other Pamunkey Chiefs had failed to do.[28] The cost; however, was great. Nor did she have any choice in the matter. No longer were Native Americans living near the Virginia Colony as independent nations. Instead, they had to live within a restricted society.

After this, she disappears from the records and dies around July 1, 1686.[29] Captain John West also vanishes from the documentation.

---

[25] Library of Virginia, *Document 5, Native American Folder* (Richmond, Virginia: Library of Virginia),1-2.

[26] Library of Virginia, *Document 5, Native American Folder* (Richmond, Virginia: Library of Virginia), 2.

[27] Library of Virginia, *Document 5, Native American Folder* (Richmond, Virginia: Library of Virginia), 5.

[28] Thomas H. Appleton, *Search for Their Places: Women in the South Across Four Centuries* (Columba and London: University of Missouri Press, 2003), 33, *GoogleBooks* (http://www.books.google.com: accessed 2 August 2017).

[29] Gregory A. Waselkov, Peter H. Wood, Thomas Hatley, *Powhatan's Mantle: Indians in the Colonial Southeast*, 259.

Children

The Children of Cockacoeske and Colonial John West are as follows:

- Captain John West, born in Virginia around 1656; time and date of death in Virginia, unknown.

Conclusion

The Native Americans of early colonial Virginia began as a powerful, all-encompassing nation. However, as early as 1656, their population and influence had declined. Disease, war, and the theft of their land made them subservient to the English crown.

Inheriting the Pamunkey chiefdom in 1656, the Queen of the Pamunkey had entered a new era of politics. Now dependent on the English government, she had to tend to the needs of her people while promoting a constructive relationship with England. Employing clever political and social tactics, she was able to create a peace between the tribes and the English. This new peace; however, was not perfect.

- A descendent of Opechancanough, the last chief to have authority over a large number of tribes, Cockacoeske's youth was surrounded by war and political strife.[30]
- Provoked by the English economic policies of encroaching on Native American lands to plant tobacco, Opechancanough led an attack on the English colonies on March 22, 1622.[31]
- Cockacoeske grew up in an era where the English settlers had a policy of forcing Christianity on Native Americans, thus creating more tension.[32]

---

[30] Charles McLean Andrews, *Narratives of the Insurrections, 1675-1690* (New York, New York: Charles Scribner's Sons, 1915), 25, Google books (Books.google.com: accessed 2 August 2017).

[31] James Douglas Rice, *Encyclopedia Virginia*, "Second Anglo-Powhatan War (1622-1632)."

[32] William Waller Hening, *The Statues at Large: Volume 1*, 114.

- Undermining their trade, economy, and stability, the English raided their corn fields and conspired to break up the Powhatan alliance in retaliation.[33]

- In 1644, Opechancanough led another major attack on Jamestown, but withdrew for unknown reasons.[34]

- By 1646, Cockacoeske had learned about Opechcanough's death in a Jamestown prison cell.[35] By now she was probably of age to learn from his mistakes.

- Necotowance inherits the chiefdom of the Pamunkey alliance, and on October 1646, he signs a peace treaty that acknowledged the end of Native American independence in Virginia.[36]

- After the death of her husband, Totopotomoy, in 1656, Cockcaoeske becomes Queen of the Pamunkey.[37]

- To foster a positive relationship with the English settlers, Cockacoeske gives birth to a child, Captain John West.[38] The father was also likely named John West.[39]

- Appearing before a committee of Indian affairs in 1676, she is asked for help against another Indian tribe but refuses. Furious that they didn't compensate her for Totopotomoy's death,[40] she storms out of the meeting.

- Attacked by Nathaniel Bacon and his rebels in 1676, the Queen of the Pamunkey flees from her land.[41]

- Signing the Peace Treaty of Middle Plantation in 1677, she legally gets the Virginia Indians to again become subordinates of the Paunkey tribe. Peace with the English is also established.[42]

---

[33] Susan Myra Kingsbury, ed., *The Records of the Virginia Company of London*, 507.

[34] Gregory A. Waselkov, Peter H. Wood, Thomas Hatley, *Powhatan's Mantle: Indians in the Colonial Southeast*, 244.

[35] Gregory A. Waselkov, Peter H. Wood, Thomas Hatley, *Powhatan's Mantle: Indians in the Colonial Southeast*, 245.

[36] William Waller Hening, *The Statues at Large: Volume 1*, 326

[37] Gregory A. Waselkov, Peter H. Wood, Thomas Hatley, *Powhatan's Mantle: Indians in the Colonial Southeast*, 245.

[38] Library of Virginia, *Document 5, Native American Folder*, 7.

[39] Library of Virginia, *Document 1, Native American Folder*, 1.

[40] Charles McLean Andrews, *Narratives of the Insurrections, 1675-1690*, 26.

[41] Charles McLean Andrews, *Narratives of the Insurrections, 1675-1690*, 127.

[42] Library of Virginia, *Document 5, Native American Folder*, 5.

- As a sign of loyalty to the English Crown, she receives a crown inscribed with *"The Queene of the Pamunkey."*[43]

---

[43] Thomas H. Appleton, *Search for Their Places: Women in the South Across Four Centuries*, 33.

Chapter 5
Thomas Joyce

Included among the most noteworthy groups of pioneers in the new world are the Scots-Irish. Migrating from Pennsylvania, they were fleeing from economical, religious, and political oppression.[1][2] Although, they left their homeland with melancholy, their hardships in Northern Ireland prepared them for Virginia. To survive they braved the frontier of colonial Virginia and the dangers associated with this life. To learn about these frontiersmen, one must examine their genealogical records in correlation to how they functioned as a Scots-Irish community.

Thomas Joyce whose family line originated in Banff, Scotland, lived in Virginia during a time of change and uncertainty, especially for dissenters from the Church of England. But even as Thomas, a Presbyterian, was forced to participate in the Church of England, a migration of Scots-Irish was arriving from Pennsylvania for a better life.[3] Over time, he and his children would migrate down the east coast as far as North Carolina.[4]

---

[1] Patrick Griffin, *The People with No Name* (Princeton, New Jersey: Princeton University Press, 2001), 65.

[2] Wayland F. Dunaway, *The Scotch-Irish of Colonial Pennsylvania* (1944: reprint, Baltimore, Maryland: Genealogical Publishing Company, 2002) 28-30.

[3] Robert P. Davis, James H. Smylie, Dean K. Thompson, Ernest Trice Thompson, William Newton Todd, *Virginia Presbyterians in American Life* (Richmond, Virginia: Hanover Presbytery, 1982), 18-19.

[4] Larry J Hoefling, *Scots and the Scotch Irish* (Oklahoma: Inlandia Press, 2009), 19.

Thomas Joyce birth date and location is unknown; died 1780 in Charlotte County, Virginia. The name of Thomas's wife is not known and the date of marriage is also unknown.

Thomas's Parentage

Thomas Joyce is first recorded in Louisa County, Virginia, with no known parents. Nor is his place of birth known; however, y-DNA evidence points to Banff, Scotland as his country of origin. David Joyce, a Thomas Joyce descendent, matches Daniel Joss, a descendent of Walter Joss, b. March 22, 1806 in Banffshire, Macduff, Scotland, at 67 markers.[5, 6] This is an indication of a direct male ancestor within a recent genealogical time frame. They also share a mutation called R-Y7729 that originates from a male ancestor that originated about 550 years ago. When the Y-DNA evidence is combined with the traditional genealogical evidence, one can see that Thomas Joyce was of Scots-Irish origin.

Life Story

Thomas appears in Louisa County, Virginia, on July 28, 1747.[7] Recorded as having a *"negro slave girl,"* adjudged to be twelve years of age, Thomas is documented as being *"of this county"*. Because his brother, Alexander, was associated with a community comprised of English and Scottish land owners, we can conclude that Thomas was involved as well.[8, 9] How Thomas became involved is unknown; however, his Scots-Irish upbringing impressed upon him the importance of hard work, and a sense of pride for his Presbyterian faith.

---

[5] Family Tree DNA, database (http://www.familytreedna.com: accessed August 15 2016), "Comparative y-DNA results" for users David Joyce and Daniel Joss" matching 67-markers, SNP R-Y7729.

[6] National Maritime Museum, "Masters and Mates Certificates, 1850-1927," database, *Ancesry.com* (www.Ancestry.com: accessed August 15 2016), entry for Walter Joss, 22 March 1806; citing Master's Certificate of Service, license no. 41.790.

[7] Louisa County, Virginia, "Louisa County, Virginia, Order Book 1, 1744-1748", p. 235, Thomas Joyce Entry, July 28 1747; Library of Virginia microfilm 29.

[8] Louisa County, Virginia," Louisa County, Virginia, Deed Book A and B, 1742-1759", part 2: p. 326, Thomas Hackett to George Clark entry, 15 August 1748; Library of Virginia microfilm 1.

[9] Louisa County Virginia," Louisa County, Virginia, Deed Book A and B, 1742-1759", Part 1: p. 89, John Thomson to Andrew Roe entry, March 9 1742/3; Library of Virginia microfilm 1.

Thomas knew about the troubles in Northern Ireland involving the Presbyterian Church and the controversies surrounding it. A dissenter from the Church of England, Thomas and Alexander, his brother, worshipped in private or along with like-minded people. Although, considered illegal, Thomas and his family kept true to their religion. As an adult Thomas also refused to attend his local parish in Louisa County.

This isolation from the Anglican community must have been hard on Thomas since Presbyterians were distrusted by Anglicans. Not only was he shunned by his Anglican neighbors, he also began forming friendships with his Scots-Irish neighbors.[10] This encouraged him to align himself with Scots-Irish and Scottish ideals, including the adaption of a clannish mentality.

During this time, Thomas also survived by living on the outskirts of civilization. With Virginia still in its youth, there were several challenges to be met. One of the most dangerous situations was the danger of Indian attacks, especially during the French and Indian War. From the beginning of the Virginia Colony, the culture clash between the European settlers and Native Americans had always been complicated. This led to armed conflicts between the two groups as early as the founding of the tidewater settlements.[11] In adulthood, Thomas supported his Scots-Irish community by supplying wagon supplies for the French and Indian War after Indian attacks increased.[12] The raids became so severe that *"whole families were being wiped out, or some*

---

[10] Dr Linda E Connors, Dr. Mary Lu MacDonald, *National Identity in Great Britain and North America, 1815-1851* (Burlington, Vermont: Ashgate Publishing Company, 2013), 75; digital images, Google Books (http://www.books.google.com: accessed 4 October 2016).

[11] Robert P. Davis, James H. Smylie, Dean K. Thompson, Ernest Trice Thompson, William Newton Todd, *Virginia Presbyterians in American Life* (Richmond, Virginia: Hanover Presbytery, 1982), 5.

[12] William Fletcher Boogher, *Gleanings of Virginia History: An Historical and Genealogical Collection, largely from Original sources* (Washington D.C.: 1903), 94; digital images, Google Books (http://www.books.google.com: accessed 5 October, 2016).

killed and the rest taken captive."[13] Some settlers even moved to more civilized regions. As a result, Scots-Irish communities formed local militias for protection.[14]

Early on, Thomas also knew about hard work. Frontier life wasn't for the faint of heart. Living so far away from the capital of Virginia, Williamsburg, Thomas was familiar with the illegal practice of land squatting. With free land for the taking, and with no formal system of purchasing land on the frontier, customary laws were established. As a witness to this system, he also likely participated in it by constructing a homestead. One can imagine Thomas planting a field of corn to establish a "*corn right*" to legally claim one hundred acres of land.[15] After which he would chop down trees and mark them to institute a "*tomahawk right*" to specify where his property lines lay.[16] To build a cabin, he would create a "*cabin right*" on which they could build a log cabin.[17]

These hardships molded Thomas into a typical Scots-Irish settler who fiercely defended his Presbyterian faith, independence, and his community. Over time, there arose new land opportunities south of Louisa County in Brunswick County, Virginia, as the Scots-Irish migration from Pennsylvania pushed southward.[18]

On January 1, 1745, John Caldwell, a Presbyterian elder, purchased 1400 acres of land in Brunswick County, Virginia, which later broke off into Lunenburg County.[19] On May 10, 1748, Thomas Joyce

[13] Robert P. Davis, James H. Smylie, Dean K. Thompson, Ernest Trice Thompson, William Newton Todd, *Virginia Presbyterians in American Life* (Richmond, Virginia: Hanover Presbytery, 1982), 33.

[14] Larry J Hoefling, *Scots and the Scotch Irish* (Oklahoma: Inlandia Press, 2009), 31.

[15] Larry J Hoefling, *Scots and the Scotch Irish* (Oklahoma: Inlandia Press, 2009), 24.

[16] Larry J Hoefling, *Scots and the Scotch Irish*, 24.

[17] Larry J Hoefling, *Scots and the Scotch Irish*, 24.

[18] Davis, Smylie, Thompson, Thompson, Todd, *Virginia Presbyterians in American Life*, 18-19.

[19] Brunswick County, Virginia," Brunswick County, Virginia, Deed Book 4, 1750-1674", p. 65-68, Kennon to Caldwell entry, 1 January 1745; Library of Virginia microfilm 3.

purchased 400 acres of land in Lunenburg County, and joined the Scots-Irish, Cub Creek community of John Caldwell.[20]

Founded as a Presbyterian settlement on the southern frontier of Virginia, Thomas was proud to being part of such a historical moment. He also understood the effort it took to get permission from Lieutenant Governor William Gooch of Virginia to legally establish a nonconformist community. On November 4, 1738, Governor Gooch allowed John Caldwell to move down with his congregation to Brunswick County.[21]

Thomas Joyce knew the Caldwell Family as is documented by the records of Cub Creek. William Caldwell, son of John Caldwell, held a position of authority in Cub Creek and was responsible for maintaining a tithable list.[22] Thomas is listed under William Caldwell's tithable list in 1752 which is an indicator that Thomas had a relationship with William Caldwell.[23] Thomas is also documented with John Caldwell in 1756 when he is listed with John Caldwell as donating supplies for "*waggonage*" during the French and Indian war.[24]

Thomas Joyce and his unknown wife had a total of 10 children, with 5 sons and 5 daughters. On 1780 Thomas passed away in Charlotte County, Virginia, and recorded the names of his children in his will.[25] Alexander, Andrew, George, Isaac, and John Joyce were included among his sons, and Elizabeth, Esther, Hannah, Mary, and Sarah Joyce were included among his daughters. Like other Scots-Irish descendants, Thomas's children also migrated into North Carolina for new land opportunities.

---

[20] Lunenburg County, Virginia, "Lunenburg County, Virginia, Deed Book 1 & 2, 1746-1752", Part 1: P.367-369, Alexander Spalding and JohnLidderdale and Samuel Gordon to Thomas Joyce entry, May 10 1748; Library of Virginia microfilm 1.

[21] Robert P. Davis, James H. Smylie, Dean K. Thompson, Ernest Trice Thompson, William Newton Todd, *Virginia Presbyterians in American Life* (Richmond, Virginia: Hanover Presbytery, 1982), 12.

[22] Brunswick County, Virginia," Brunswick County, Virginia, Deed Book 4, 1750-1674", p. 58-59, Kennon to Caldwell entry, 1 January 1745; Library of Virginia microfilm 3.

[23] Lunenburg County, Virginia, "Lunenburg County, Virginia, Tithable Lists, 1748-1756", Thomas Joyce Entry, 1752; Library of Virginia microfilm 422.

[24] Boogher, *Gleanings of Virginia History: An Historical and Genealogical Collection*, 94.

[25] Charlotte County, Virginia, "Charlotte County, Virginia, Will Book 1, 1765—1791," p. 221-222, T. Joyce's Will, 1 June 1780; Microfilm 16.

Children

The children of Thomas Joyce and his unknown wife are as follows:

- ALEXANDER JOYCE, born in Lunenburg County or Charlotte County, Virginia; died after December 28, 1817 when he wrote his will.[26] He married Mary Smith.[27]

- ANDREW JOYCE, born January 20, 1771, probably in Charlotte County, Virginia; died April 30, 1853 in Patrick County, Virginia.[28] He married Nancy Ann Burye.[29]

- ELIZABETH (JOYCE) JOHNSTON, probably born in Charlotte County, Virginia. In Thomas's will she is referred to as Elizabeth Johnston.[30]

- ESTHER (JOYCE) SHIPP, probably born in Charlotte County ca 1770, Virginia; died in Marshall County, Mississippi. She married Josiah Shipp on April 13 1790 in Strokes County, North Carolina.[31]

- GEORGE JOYCE, born October 18, 1759 in Lunenburg County, Virginia; died September 15, 1835 in Bullitt Kentucky.[32, 33]

---

[26] Strokes County, North Carolina, Records Wills No. 3, 1816-1836, "Alexander Joyce Entry," 28 December 1817; digital image, Ancestry (http://www.ancestry.com: accessed 8 October 2016); Corinne Johnson Murray, *The Joyces* (Greensboro, North Carolina), 71.

[27] Murray, *The Joyces*, 71.

[28] Corinne Johnson Murray, *The Joyces* (Greensboro, North Carolina), 81.

[29] Murray, *The Joyces*, 81.

[30] Strokes Co., North Carolina., Records Wills No. 3, 1816-1836: 71,"Alexander Joyce Entry," 28 December 1817; Corinne Johnson Murray, *The Joyces* (Greensboro, North Carolina), 97.

[31] Corinne Johnson Murray, *The Joyces* (Greensboro, North Carolina), 93-96; contains transcriptions of original documents from Hickman County, Tennessee, and Marshall County, Mississippi; Charlotte Co., "Charlotte County, Virginia, Will Book 1, 1765—1791," p. 221-222.

[32] Corinne Johnson Murray, *The Joyces* (Greensboro, North Carolina), 69-70; contains a transcription of George Joyce's pension application request; Kentucky, "Pension Payment Roll of Veterans of the Revolutionary War and the Regular Army and Navy, 3/1801 - 9/1815," p. 237, George Joyce, Died 15d September 1835; digital image, Ancestry (http://www.ancestry.com: accessed 9 October 2016).

[33] Murray, *The Joyces, 69-70.*

- HANNAH (JOYCE) SHIPP, probably born ca 1750 in Lunenburg County, Virginia.[34] She married Thomas Shipp of North Carolina.[35]

- ISAAC JOYCE, probably born in Charlotte County, Virginia; died intestate on January 4, 1831 in Strokes County, North Carolina.[36] He married Elizabeth Smith, the sister of Mary Smith.[37]

- JOHN JOYCE, probably born in Charlotte County, Virginia; died intestate in 1815 in Rockingham County, North Carolina.[38] He married Peggy, surname unknown.[39]

- MARY (JOYCE) CARDWELL, born August 21, 1747, probably in Lunenburg County, Virginia; died May 15, 1824 in North Carolina.[40] She married Thomas Cardwell of Charlotte County, Virginia.[41]

- SARAH (JOYCE) MARSHALL, born in Lunenburg or Charlotte County, Virginia. She married John Marshall or Thomas Marshall.[42]

---

[34] Charlotte Co., "Charlotte County, Virginia, Will Book 1, 1765—1791," p. 221-222; Corinne Johnson Murray, *The Joyces* (Greensboro, North Carolina), 83-87; contains a transcription of Thomas Shipp's pension application request.

[35] Charlotte Co., "Charlotte County, Virginia, Will Book 1, 1765—1791," p. 221-222; Murray, *The Joyces, 83-87;* contains a transcription of Thomas Shipp's pension application request.

[36] Strokes County, North Carolina, Probate Records, 1753-1971 ; Indexes 1753-1965, Joyce, Isaac; District and Probate Courts, North Carolina; digital image, Ancestry.com (http://www.ancestry.com: accessed 9 October 2016).

[37] Strokes County, North Carolina, North Carolina, Wills and Probate Records,1665-1998, "William Smith Will," 1 October 1795; digital image, Ancestry.com (http://www.ancestry.com: accessed 9 October 2016), 43.

[38] Rockingam County, North Carolina, Wills, 1663-1978; Estate Papers, 1780-1926, Joyce, John; District and Probate Courts, North Carolina; digital image, Ancestry (http://www.ancestry.com: accessed 9 October 2016).

[39] Corinne Johnson Murray, *The Joyces* (Greensboro, North Carolina), 30.

[40] Cardwell/Clark Family Bible, *Thomas Cardwell Bible*; privately held by Mrs. Jennie Clark Hawkins. Information is included that Mary Joyce was born August 21, 1747, and died May 15, 1824. Information is also included that she married Thomas Cardwell married Mary Joyce; digital image, Ancestry (http://www.ancestry.com: accessed 10 October 2016).

[41] Cardwell/Clark Family Bible, *Thomas Cardwell Bible*; Charlotte Co., "Charlotte County, Virginia, Will Book 1, 1765—1791," p. 221-222; Murray, *The Joyces, 97.*

[42] Murray, *The Joyces, 97;* Charlotte Co., "Charlotte County, Virginia, Will Book 1, 1765—1791," p. 221-222.

Conclusion

In order to confirm that Thomas Joyce of central and southern Virginia
was of Scots-Irish origins, one must prove he had Scottish ancestors.
Based on y-DNA evidence and traditional genealogical evidence, we
can reach this conclusion.

- David Joyce, a Thomas Joyce descendent, matches Daniel Joss
  whose line comes from Banffshire, Macduff, Scotland, at 67-
  markers which is a strong indication of a common male
  ancestor within a genealogical time frame.[43] They also share a
  SNP or mutation in their y-DNA from a common direct male
  ancestor which is estimated to be 550 years old.[44]

- On July 28, 1747, Thomas is recorded in Louisa County,
  Virginia, as being "*of this county*" and as having the age of a
  "*negro slave girl*" adjudged to be twelve years of age.[45] On
  August 15, 1748, his brother, Alexander Joyce, was
  associated with the same influential community.[46]

- On May 10, 1748, Thomas purchased 400 acres of land in
  Lunenburg County, Virginia, to join a Scots-Irish settlement led
  by John Caldwell.[47] On January 1, 1745, John Caldwell
  purchased 1400 acres of land in Brunswick which turned into
  Lunenburg County in 1746.[48]

- In 1752, Thomas is listed under William Caldwell's tithable
  list, and in March 1756, he is recorded as donating
  "*waggonage*" for the French and Indian War along

---

[43] FamilyTreeDNA, August 15 2016, "Comparative y-DNA results" for users David Joyce
and Daniel Joss", SNP R-Y7729.

[44] FamilyTreeDNA, August 15 2016, "Comparative y-DNA results" for users David Joyce
and Daniel Joss", SNP R-Y7729.

[45] Louisa County, Virginia, Order Book 1: 235.

[46] Louisa County, Virginia, Deed Book B: 326; Louisa County, Virginia, Deed Book A: 89.

[47] Lunenburg County, Virginia, Deed Book 1: 367-369.

[48] Brunswick County, Virginia, Deed Book 4: 65-68.

with John Caldwell.[49] This documentation when correlated with the y-DNA confirms that they shared cultural interests.

[49] Lunenburg County, Virginia, Tithable Lists, Entry for Thomas Joyce, 1752;Boogher, *Gleanings of Virginia History: An Historical and Genealogical Collection*, 94.

Chapter 6
Thomas Stanley

The history of religious tolerance stems from a complicated, dark period in American history. Once the only legally established Christian denomination in Virginia, the Church of England held supreme political power. With Church and State intertwined, the colonial government could tax and jail those who opposed the Church of England. This policy, imposed on religious dissenters, planted the seeds for the American Revolution.

Thomas Stanley's struggle with the English establishment was one that was experienced by other dissenting Christians. Born into the Church of England, he left this denomination to join the Society of Friends. As a new member of the Quakers, he became accustomed to the rules that he was expected to follow. Radically different from the culture associated with the Anglican Church, the life Thomas adapted was misunderstood by outsiders. As a result, he was a witness to the religious persecution that often befell his fellow Quakers. However, his participation in the Society of Friends influenced other Anglicans to rebel against the Church of England.

Thomas Stanley: Probably born abt. 1660; died abt. 1733 in New Kent County, Virginia.

Thomas's Parentage: The parents of Thomas Stanley are not known; however, based on Thomas's participation in the Church of England, it is probable that Thomas's parents were Anglicans. As members of traditional English society, they were familiar with the duties accompanying it, and raised Thomas to be an Anglican.

Life Story: The story of Thomas Stanley begins in New Kent County, Virginia, in St. Peter's Parish. First documented as clearing a road for Alexander MacKeney on December 18, 1697,[1] he was responsible for expanding the colony. With no separation of Church and State, Anglican parishes were required to oversee the building and repairing of roads.[2] As the leader of a *"gang"* or group or workers, he was essential to the functionality of New Kent County.[3]

The following year on April 15, 1688, James Stanley, first son of Thomas Stanley, was baptized.[4] Later on November 23, 1689, his second son, Thomas, was baptized.[5] However, it wasn't until the baptism of his third son, John, on October 11, 1691 that he considered leaving the Church of England.[6] Two months later, an incident in St. Peter's Parish forever changed Thomas Stanley's life.

James Dickinson, a renowned Quaker, challenged Thomas Stanley's views on religion. Holding a meeting at Blackcreak in New Kent County, the theology James taught ultimately caught the attention of local authorities. Considered *"the radicals of the Protestant Reformation,"*[7] their cultural practices were different from the other religious dissenters.

It is not known if Thomas Stanley was personally there to witness James Dickinson's sermons, but he did hear about them. One of the differences between the Society of Friends and the Church of England was how each denomination viewed the role of government.

One example of a belief that clashed with the ideology of the Church of England was the belief that *"civil government would become less*

---

[1] St. Peter's Parish, *The Vestry Book of Saint Peter's: New Kent County, Va. from 1682-1758* (Heritage books, 2015), 42, 45.

[2] Virginia Genealogical Society, *New Kent and Hanover County [Virginia] Road Orders (1706-17430),* (Westminister, Maryland: Heritage Books, 2003), v.

[3] Virginia Genealogical Society, *New Kent and Hanover County [Virginia] Road Orders (1706-17430),* (Westminister, Maryland: Heritage Books, 2003), 101.

[4] St. Peter's Parish, *The parish register of Saint Peter's , New Kent county, Virginia from 168-1787* (Heritage Books), 35.

[5] St. Peter's Parish, *The parish register of Saint Peter's , New Kent county, Virginia from 168-1787,* 35.

[6] St. Peter's Parish, *The parish register of Saint Peter's , New Kent county, Virginia from 168-1787,* 35.

[7] J.P. Bell, *Our Quaker Friends of Ye Olden Time* (Bowie, Maryland: Heritage Books, 1905), 171.

necessary"[8] if people lived by the values of Jesus Christ.

Another important aspect of Quaker theology James Dickinson preached was based on the objection of Oaths. Discouraging people from trusting oaths, he taught that they were, *"very injurious to morality,"*[9] since the truth should only be sworn before God. Considering these ideals dangerous, the English authorities saw this as a threat to the government.

Also the taking up of arms was forbidden by the Society of Friends. While the local authorities depended on militias for their defense, the Quakers considered it *"unlawful for christians to engage in the profession of arms."*[10] Preferring to live a life like Jesus Christ and avoiding any form of mandatory recruitment, they were fined and even risked imprisonment.

The disagreements between the Quakers and the Church of England did not end there. Believing that Christians should preach for spiritual rewards instead of receiving money,[11] they looked down on Anglican Rectors. While ministers associated with the Church of England depended on tithes for their livelihood, the Quaker's resistance to paying these taxes was deemed as a threat.

In addition to being inspired by the words of James Dickinson, Thomas Stanley also knew about the sufferings James had endured. Questioned by the sheriff on *"whose authority,"* he had come to preach, James responded, *"in the authority of the great God, to whom we muft give an Account."*[12] After being commanded to leave, James convinced the sheriff to allow him to quietly proceed with his meeting.

---

[8] J.P. Bell, *Our Quaker Friends of Ye Olden Time* (Bowie, Maryland: Heritage Books, 1905), 200.

[9] J.P. Bell, *Our Quaker Friends of Ye Olden Time* (Bowie, Maryland: Heritage Books, 1905), 205.

[10] J.P. Bell, *Our Quaker Friends of Ye Olden Time* (Bowie, Maryland: Heritage Books, 1905), 206.

[11] J.P. Bell, *Our Quaker Friends of Ye Olden Time* (Bowie, Maryland: Heritage Books, 1905), 212.

[12] James Dickinson, *A Journal of the Life, Travels and Labour of Love in the Work of the Ministry, of that Worthly Elder and Faithful Servant of Jesus Christ, James Dickinfon* (London, England: Bible in Georgeyard, 1745), 54; digital images, *Google Books* (http://www.books.google.com: accessed 20 11 2017).

The aftermath of James Dickinson's visit; although tragic by modern standards, was still successful. Thomas Stanley and several other members of St. Peter's Parish decided to leave the Church of England to join the Society of Friends. However, the cost was great, and it exposed them to harsh punishments.

First appearing in New Kent County on March 10, 1700 as a witness to a Quaker marriage between Thomas Lankford and Martha West,[13] Thomas Stanley had joined the Society of Friends. As a new member, he realized that his friends and in-laws no longer wanted to be associated with him, nor could they if they desired too. The stigma attached to the Society of Friends was so deeply embed in society that anyone who had a relationship with them was shunned.

To worship as he pleased, Thomas Stanley was required to swear an oath of allegiance, declaring that he would be *"faithful to King William and Queen Mary"*[14], and that he would *"for evermore"* put faith in God and in Jesus Christ.[15] While this applied to other dissenting denominations, it violated a core belief of the Quakers that oaths between men were unethical.

Thomas Stanley was also aware that places of worship for dissenters had to be approved by the Church of England.[16] Knowing that his fellow Quakers never took the oaths of allegiance, he understood that there would never be a legal place of worship. As result, he and the Quaker community worshiped in secret, even at the risk of being fined and jailed.[17]

As Thomas met in the shadows with his colleagues, he had gotten into trouble with his new neighbors as well. In 1706, he was *"accused of*

[13] F. Edward Wright, *Quaker Records of Henrico Monthly Meeting* (Lewes, Delaware: Colonial Roots, 2012), 1.

[14] University of Wisconsin, *Act of Toleration, May 1689* (Wisconsin: University of Wisconsin), 1-2; digital images, *University of Wisconsin* (https://www.ssc.wisc.edu/~rkeyser/wp/wp-content/uploads/2015/06/TolerationAct1689.pdf: accessed 21 11 2017).

[15] University of Wisconsin, *Act of Toleration, May 1689*, 1-2.

[16] Robert P. Davis, James H. Smylie, Dean K. Thompson, Ernest Trice Thompson, William Newton Todd, *Virginia Presbyterians in American Life* (Richmond, Virginia: Hanover Presbytery, 1982), 27.

[17] University of Wisconsin, *Act of Toleration, May 1689*, 1-2; Davis, Smylie, Thompson, Thompson, Todd, *Virginia Presbyterians in American Life*, 27.

being overtaken with drunkenness."[18] Later on November 18, 1706, Thomas apologized;[19] however, his involvement with the Anglican Church was not completely abolished.

On December 16, 1714, Thomas Stanley and his son, Thomas Stanley, Junior, were granted 800 acres of land in New Kent County for importing sixteen persons to Virginia.[20] However, his decision to accept a government grant was not out of disobedience, but rather, it was out of necessity. In 1722 Thomas donated this land to help build the Cedar Creek meetinghouse in Hanover County, Virginia.[21] Contributing funds to its construction on June 5 1722,[22] he earned a controversial reputation. Although, he had proven himself to be a faithful member of the Society of Friends, it is probable that he also had minor disagreements with them.

Two years later on June 1, 1724, Thomas Stanley *"brought before the meeting a woman, not being a friend, declared his intentions of taking a wife."*[23] It is not known how his request was accepted, but based on the known evidence, it did not go well. Later in 1724, Thomas *"condemned"* his ambition to marry an outsider.[24]

Ironically, this was a common occurrence within the Society of Friends. Those who broke the laws and customs of the Quakers risked being disowned.[25] It is not known why Thomas Stanley disobeyed these rules, but two years later he once again had gotten

---

[18] F. Edward Wright, *Quaker Records of Henrico Monthly Meeting* (Lewes, Delaware: Colonial Roots, 2012), 5.

[19] Wright, *Quaker Records of Henrico Monthly Meeting*, 5.

[20] "Online Catalog: Images & indexes," database with images, *The Library of Virginia* (http://lva1.hosted.exlibrisgroup.com: accessed 21 November 2017), Thomas Standley, senr, 16 December 1714, 800 acres, Virginia, Colonial Land Office, Patents, 1623-1774; Library of Virginia; information supplied by the National Stanley Family Association.

[21] Information also provided by the National Stanley Family Association.

[22] F. Edward Wright, *Quaker Records of Henrico Monthly Meeting* (Lewes, Delaware: Colonial Roots, 2012), 11-12.

[23] F. Edward Wright, *Quaker Records of Henrico Monthly Meeting* (Lewes, Delaware: Colonial Roots, 2012), 13.

[24] F. Edward Wright, *Quaker Records of Henrico Monthly Meeting* (Lewes, Delaware: Colonial Roots, 2012), 14.

[25] J.P. Bell, *Our Quaker Friends of Ye Olden Time* (Bowie, Maryland: Heritage Books, 1905), 145.

himself into trouble. Coming before the Quaker authorities, Thomas had *"taken a wife not of our society,"*[26] and was *"publickly drunk."*[27]

Whatever Thomas's reasons for being disobedient, beginning on July 3, 1720, he was ordered to build a road from Ceder Creek to new market Mill for the English Government.[28] Under the instructions of St. Peter's Parish, he was also directed to clear additional roads in 1722 and 1735.[29] Why Thomas built roads for St. Peter's Parish is unknown, but it is probable that he had no choice. Under pressure from the Church of England, he had to comply.

On July 7, 1733, Thomas Stanley's involvement with the Anglican Church affected his life as a Quaker. After trying to fit in both worlds for the betterment of his brethren and out of necessity for the Anglican Church, he would pay dearly. Forced to give a horse as tithes to St. Peter's Parish,[30] he paid the price for abandoning his former associates. Not only had he personally suffered, but his son, James Stanley, had to forfeit eight sheep.[31]

The price they paid was heavy. Aware that horses in Virginia were highly-valued for both transportation and for monetary value, the English wanted James Stanley to suffer. The penalty for James Stanley was far worse. As a farmer, James depended on his life stock, and the loss of eight sheep hurt him economically.

Disappearing from the Quaker and Anglican records, it is probable that Thomas Stanley died around 1735. The life he lived; however, was not uncommon for members of the Society of Friends. Often forced to serve

---

[26] F. Edward Wright, *Quaker Records of Henrico Monthly Meeting* (Lewes, Delaware: Colonial Roots, 2012), 15.

[27] Edward Wright, *Quaker Records of Henrico Monthly Meeting*, 15.

[28] Virginia Genealogical Society, *New Kent and Hanover County [Virginia] Road Orders (1706-17430)*, (Westminster, Maryland: Heritage Books, 2003), 7.

[29] Virginia Genealogical Society, *New Kent and Hanover County [Virginia] Road Orders (1706-17430)*, (Westminster, Maryland: Heritage Books, 2003), 8,12.

[30] F. Edward Wright, *Quaker Records of Henrico Monthly Meeting* (Lewes, Delaware: Colonial Roots, 2012), 17.

[31] Wright, *Quaker Records of Henrico Monthly Meeting*, 17.

both the Anglican Church and the Quaker Church, they faced the consequences. Their sufferings; fortunately, were not in vain.

The established Church of England had not only intruded on the rights of Quakers, but it penalized the Presbyterians and Baptists as well. The discontent caused by the Anglican Church's policies became one of the motivations for the American Revolution. Despite all their hardships, men like Thomas Stanley played an important role in Virginia, even if they are not recorded in the history books.

Children

The Children of Thomas Stanley are as follows:

- JAMES STANLEY, born April 16, 1688 in New Kent County, Virginia;[32] died 1754 in Hanover County. Virginia. He married Catherine Hutchinson on March 5, 1728.[33]

- THOMAS STANLEY, born November 23, 1689 in New Kent County, Virginia;[34] death date unknown. He married 1st Elizabeth Maddox in 1714.[35] He married 2nd Elizabeth Crew on October 1726.[36]

- JOHN STANLEY, born Oct 11, 1691 in New Kent County, Virginia;[37] died July 11, 1783 in Hanover County, Virginia.[38] He married 1st Allice Ballard in 1728.[39]

---

[32] St. Peter's Parish, *The Vestry Book of Saint Peter's: New Kent County, Va. from 1682-1758*, 45.

[33] F. Edward Wright, *Quaker Records of Henrico Monthly Meeting* (Lewes, Delaware: Colonial Roots, 2012), 17.

[34] St. Peter's Parish, *The Vestry Book of Saint Peter's: New Kent County, Va. from 1682-1758*, 45.

[35] Ancestry," Family Data Collection," database, *Ancestry.com* (http://www.ancestry.com: accessed 22 November 2017), entry for Thomas Stanley and Elizabeth Maddox.

[36] Society of Friends (Charles County, Virginia), "*U.S., Quaker Meeting Records, 1681-1935*," p 154, Thomas Stanley and Elizabeth Crew, 1 October 1726; digital images, *Ancestry.com* (http://www.ancestry.com: accessed 22 11 2017).

[37] St. Peter's Parish, *The Vestry Book of Saint Peter's: New Kent County, Va. from 1682-1758*, 45.

[38] Ancestry," Family Data Collection," database, *Ancestry.com* (http://www.ancestry.com: accessed 22 November 2017), entry for John Stanley, 17 July 1783.

[39] Ancestry," Family Data Collection," database, *Ancestry.com*, database (http://www.ancestry.com: accessed 22 November 2017), entry for John Stanley and Alice Ballard, 1728.

Conclusion

The Virginia Colony, considered a strong supporter of religious freedom in the War for Independence, had a controversial start. Under the direction of a Royal Governor, state and church were unified with the local parishes acting as its local representative. With the backing from the English government, the Church of England had authority at the expense of other Christian denominations.

Thomas Stanley, originally a member of the Anglican Church, decided to join the Society of Friends. His story is typical of religious dissenters in colonial Virginia and the kind of life they lived. Often forced to live in both worlds, he participated in St. Peter's Parish as a necessity.

As a member of the Quaker Church, he struggled with obeying some of their doctrines, especially with drinking and marrying outside of the society. As a result, he developed a controversial reputation despite his contribution of 800 acres of land to build the Cedar Creek Meeting House.

Although he made every attempt to live a life in harmony with both the Quaker Church and the Church of England, he found himself unable to do this. Near the end of his life, he and his family suffered at the hands of English authorities. Forced to give up a mare as a tithe to the Church of England, it is clear his loyalty was with the Society of Friends.

- On December 18, 1697, Thomas Stanley is recorded as a leader of a "*gang*" who was tasked with building a road for St. Peter's parish.[40] As a leader of a gang, he held a respectable place in traditional English society. Responsible for expanding and repairing the road system in New Kent County, Virginia,[41] he helped expand the colony.
- After hearing about the visit of James Dickinson, a visiting Quaker, Thomas Stanley left the Church of England.[42] Joining

---

[40] St. Peter's Parish, *The Vestry Book of Saint Peter's: New Kent County, Va. from 1682-1758*, 42, 45.

[41] Virginia Genealogical Society, *New Kent and Hanover County [Virginia] Road Orders (1706-17430)*, v.

[42] Dickinson, *A Journal of the Life, Travels and Labour of Love in the Work of the Ministry, of that Worthly Elder and Faithful Servant of Jesus Christ, James Dickinfon*, 54.

the Society of Friends, he was inspired by the doctrines of his new faith.

- Attracted by the ideology that civil government was not necessary if humans lived like Jesus Christ, he became disillusioned with the Established Church of England.[43] This even included the practice of taking oaths. As a member of the Society of Friends, he believed that oaths between men were, *"very injurious to morality."*[44]

- The concept of rejecting war was another tenant that proved to be important to him. As a Quaker, he preferred to live by peaceful means.[45]

- Despite his contribution of 800 acres of land on which to build Cedar Creek meetinghouse,[46] he became a controversial figure.

- In 1706, Thomas Stanley was *"accused of being overtaken with drunkenness."*[47] Later, he apologized; however, on June 1, 1724, Thomas was *"brought before the meeting a woman, not being a friend, declared his intentions of taking a wife."*[48] Deemed inappropriate by the Quaker authorities, he *"condemned"* his intention of taking a wife.[49] However, two years later, he married a woman not of the society.[50]

- On July 3, 1720, Thomas Stanley was again ordered to tend to the roads in New Kent County, Virginia.[51] The reasons; however, were out of necessity. If he did not comply, he would be fined or imprisoned.[52]

---

[43] Bell, *Our Quaker Friends of Ye Olden Time*, 200.

[44] Bell, *Our Quaker Friends of Ye Olden Time*, 205.

[45] Bell, *Our Quaker Friends of Ye Olden Time*, 206.

[46] "Online Catalog: Images & indexes," *The Library of Virginia* , Thomas Standley, senr, 16 December 1714, 800 acres, Virginia, Colonial Land Office, Patents, 1623-1774.

[47] Wright, *Quaker Records of Henrico Monthly Meeting*, 5.

[48] Wright, *Quaker Records of Henrico Monthly Meeting*, 13.

[49] Wright, *Quaker Records of Henrico Monthly Meeting*, 14.

[50] Wright, *Quaker Records of Henrico Monthly Meeting*, 15.

[51] Virginia Genealogical Society, *New Kent and Hanover County [Virginia] Road Orders*, 7.

[52] University of Wisconsin, *Act of Toleration, May 1689*, 1-2.

- Thomas's interaction with the Society of Friends was noticed by the English Authorities. On July 7, 1733, he was forced to forfeit a mare as a tithe to the Church of England.[53] Considered a valuable asset both economically and practically, it was a great loss.
- The details of his passing are unknown, but his sufferings were not in vain. Because of the stories of men like Thomas Stanley, the Virginia colony eventually gained complete religious freedom.

---

[53] Wright, *Quaker Records of Henrico Monthly Meeting*, 17.

Chapter 7
William Witcher

The modern world and its technology has conditioned us to live differently than our ancestors. In Colonial Virginia our ancestors lived by a different creed. One of these core beliefs was working more closely with your community. Whether it was participating in politics, working with the local militia, or becoming more involved in the legal system, people were more engaged with their neighbors.

An examination of the life and times of William Witcher, a middle-class planter, highlights this theme. Said to be an immigrant, the social groups and activates he became associated with depict a fulfilled life. Beginning as a common planter, he became a vestryman, a justice of the peace, and eventually a captain of the militia. Along with all these accomplishments came responsibilities to serve his community. As a result, he became a man of influence in Pittsylvania County, Virginia.

William Witcher: Born 1739; died on December 8, 1806 in Pittsylvania County, Virginia.[1] He likely married Liddy Atkins.

William's Parentage: The parents of William are unknown.

Life Story: Beginning on November 15, 1758, William Witcher is recorded as a member of Antrim Parish in Halifax County, Virginia. Already a church official, he along with William Adkerson and Richard Shockley, were ordered to process the '*bounds of every persons land from*

---

[1] Find a Grave.ˣ *Find a Grave*, database with images (http://www.findagrave.com: accessed 9 August 2017), memorial 85989311, Maj William Reuben Witcher, Sr (1739-1806), William Witcher Family Cemetery, Pittsylvania County, Virginia, gravestone photograph by Thomas K. Brigham; Lela C. Adams, *Wills of Pittsylvania County, Virginia (1767-1820)*, (Greenville, South Carolina: Southern Historical Press, 1986), 141.

Arthur Beardings up Pigg River."[2] Responsible for adding new lands to the property of the parish, he was trusted with the church's well-being.

The childhood of William Witcher is not recorded; however, due to his participation in the Church of England, one can conclude he was raised in that environment. Considered the only legal religion in Virginia, the Anglican Church also held political influence as church and state were one. As the years passed, he learned this would help him rise in society, both economically and politically.

As an English subject, he also knew about the controversial nature of the Church of England. Holding all the political power, the Anglican Church discredited other Christian denominations and forbid them to freely worship.

Presbyterians, Baptists, and Quakers willingly challenged the church's authority at the risk of being persecuted. If anyone refused to attend church services, their tithes were taxed, and they risked being jailed.[3] In this divided society, William Witcher continued to remain loyal to the Church of England.

Like most established settlers, he also was expanding his land. On July 29, 1758, he purchased 100 acres of land in Halifax County from William Adkinson.[4] Living near Pigg River, William Witcher is also documented as being a witness to five land transactions by the said River.[5]

---

[2] Marion Dodson Chiarito, Vestry Book of Antrim Parish Halifax County, Virginia (1752-1817), (Athens, Georgia: Iberian Publishing Company, 1983), 39.

[3] Robert P. Davis, James H. Smylie, Dean K. Thompson, Ernest Trice Thompson, William Newton Todd, *Virginia Presbyterians in American Life: Hanover Presbytery (1755-1980)*, (Richmond, Virginia: Hanover Presbytery, 1982), 19; Christopher C Dean, *Memoir of the Rev. Samuel Davies* (Boston, Massachusetts: Massachusetts Sabbath School Union, 1832), 16.

[4] Marion Dodson Chiarito, *Halifax County, Virginia, Deed Book 1(1752-1758)*, (1985; reprint, Athens, Georgia: Iberian Publishing Company, 1996), 39.

[5] Halifax County, Virginia, Deed Book, No. 4, (1762 – 1763): 9, 359, William Witcher; Microfilm 2; Library of Virginia, Richmond; Halifax County, Virginia, Deed Book, No 6, (1765 – 1767): 35, 100, 103, 196, William Witcher; Microfilm 3; Library of Virginia, Richmond.

Recorded later on August 26, 1768, William now living in neighboring Pittsylvania County,[6] buys 50 acres of land on Pigg River from William Adkinson.[7] An active member of his community, his business transactions were not limited to purchasing land. He also began to make a small profit by selling his property. By June 16, 1764, William Witcher had sold 623 acres of land in Pittsylvania County.[8]

The acquisition of his land wasn't by accident. Rather, it was due to his involvement in the Church of England. As a well-known member of the church, he acquired friends, acquaintances, and business contacts. However, one cannot discount how his role as Vestryman and Overseer of the Poor in Camden Parish was also equally important.

The roles of Vestrymen and Overseers of the Poor, although helpful to the Church of England, were essential in maintaining the English government. Church and state were one entity, and, as such, any official position was related to the Anglican Church.

The levying and distributing of tithes was an essential task for vestrymen. William Witcher, already viewed by the community with respect, had to decide how to use them. As a church official, he understood the purpose of the parish was to support the congregation, provide a salary for the minister, and to expand the parish. Trusted with these duties, he is recorded with paying Reverend James Stevenson *"for a salary of 3 months,"* with 4312 pounds of tobacco.[9] Another duty was to determine if the Church Wardens would *"provide necessaries for the blind children of JOHN DALTON and THOMAS SANDAGE."*[10] He even was instrumental in ordering others to add new land to the parish.

---

[6] Iberian Publishing Company, *Iberian Publish Company's On-Line Catalog: The Growth of Virginia, 1634-1895, 1651-1660* (http://genealogyresources.org/Va_map_1650.html: accessed 11 August 2017), "1767 – Pittsylvania (Halifax)."

[7] Lucille C. Payne, Neil, G. Payne, *Pittsylvania County Virginia (1765-1774)*, (Greenville, South Carolina: Southern Historical Press, Inc.,1991), 18.

[8] Lucille C. Payne, Neil, G. Payne, *Pittsylvania County Virginia (1765-1774)*, (Greenville, South Carolina: Southern Historical Press, Inc.,1991),19, 135, 137, 182.

[9] Mary Leigh Boisseau, *Vestry Book of Camden Parish (1767-1820)*, (Danville, Virginia: Mary Leigh Boisseau, 1986), 10.

[10] Mary Leigh Boisseau, *Vestry Book of Camden Parish (1767-1820)*, (Danville, Virginia: Mary Leigh Boisseau, 1986), 11.

An example is when at a vestry he ordered, *"JOHN WHEELER, WILLIAM COLLIER, and THOMAS COLLIER procession all the patent land from the OLD WOMAN'S CREEK up STANTON RIVER to PIGG RIVER, thence up PIGG RIVER to the FRYING PAN CREEK."*[11]

As an Overseer of the Poor, William Witcher helped those suffering from unfortunate circumstances. Beginning on September 1, 1788, he decided if John Goings should receive 2000 pounds of tobacco for supporting Ann Going.[12] In another case, Daniel Hankins received 320 pounds of tobacco *"for furnishing JOHN BLANKINGSHIP 2 barrels corn & 100 1lbs. pork."* [13] He even assisted in educating apprentices like James Southerland, so that *"he will teach and instruct to read and write the said James Southerland,"* so that James *"may get a livelihood."*[14]

Over the years, as William Witcher ordered more lands to be processed, he also saw Anglo-Indian relations worsen. As Native American lands were being taken away by frontier families, peace treaties were being negotiated; however, they were only temporary solutions. Finally, in August 1774, the Choctaw, Shawnee, and Delaware Indians attacked families along Sinking Creek in southern Pittsylvania County.[15] In retaliation, Governor Lord Dunmore commanded General Andrew Lewis to confront the Indian collation.[16]

There is no documentation if William Witcher participated in Lord Dunmore's War, but the aftermath affected William for years to come. After the surrender of the Native Americans on October 10, 1774, it

---

[11] Mary Leigh Boisseau, *Vestry Book of Camden Parish (1767-1820)*, (Danville, Virginia: Mary Leigh Boisseau, 1986), 13.

[12] Mary Leigh Boisseau, *Vestry Book of Camden Parish (1767-1820)*, (Danville, Virginia: Mary Leigh Boisseau, 1986), 51.

[13] Mary Leigh Boisseau, *Vestry Book of Camden Parish (1767-1820)*, (Danville, Virginia: Mary Leigh Boisseau, 1986), 66.

[14] Gayle Austin, *Abstracts of Pittsylvania County, VA. Deeds (1783-1790)*, (Greenville, South Carolina: Southern Historical Press, Inc., 2007), 145-146.

[15] Larry G. Aaron, *Pittsylvania County Virginia: A Brief History* (Charleston, South Carolina: The History Press, 2009), 49.

[16] Aaron, *Pittsylvania County Virginia: A Brief History*, 49.

became clear that more protective measures had to be implemented.[17]

On February 11, 1775, William was elected by his contemporaries to the Committee of Safety of Pittsylvania County. Composed of thirty-one men, only the most respected were allowed to join. Founded on *"defending their liberties and properties, at the risk of their lives, and if required, to die by their fellow suffers [the Bostonians],"*[18] they were now responsible for securing the frontier. Under the direction of the Virginia Convention, the Committee of Safety assembled two regiments of one thousand men each. Serving under Major John Wilson, William Witcher was appointed a Captain on September 27, 1775.[19]

In addition to providing protection against aggressive Native Americans, William's regiment was also formed for patriotic reasons. Intended as support for General George Washington's Northern Army, William had to be ready if called upon.[20]

By now, the Anglican Church's influence and power had weakened. Due to ant-British aspirations and the rise of the Presbyterian, Baptist, Quaker, and Methodist denominations, loyal Englishmen and women had abandoned the Church of England. However, by examining William Witcher's participation in Camden Parish, we learn that this relationship was not always predictable.

As a vestryman, he remained faithful to the Anglican faith despite being a member of the Committee of Safety. It is unknown why he decided to remain a vestryman after the American Revolution. Perhaps he was being politically savvy. Whatever the case, there must have been some conflicted emotions involved.

The same year of Lord Dunmore's War, William Witcher was appointed a justice of the peace for Pittsylvania County. Under the authority of the

[17] Larry G. Aaron, *Pittsylvania County Virginia: A Brief History* (Charleston, South Carolina: The History Press, 2009), 50.

[18] Aaraon, *Pittsylvania County Virginia: A Brief History*, 50.

[19] Virginia Historical Society, *The Virginia Magazine of History and Biography* (Richmond, Virginia: Virginia Historical Society, 1911), 307; digital images, *Internet Archive* (http://www.archive.org: accessed 12 August 2017).

[20] Aaraon, *Pittsylvania County Virginia: A Brief History*, 50.

Governor of Virginia, he was again tasked with duties contrary to the purpose of the Committee of Safety.

Dissimilar to the vow he took to defend *"their liberties and properties, at the risk of their lives* [against England],"[21] he was also responsible for overseeing *"cases of profanity, fornication, and unnecessary absence of Church."*[22] This conflict of interest put him in a position where he imposed tithes on religious dissenters.

In July 1776, William Witcher's patriotic loyalty was tested. Convinced by British agents to raid the frontier, Native Americans had forced these Virginians to live in crowded forts.[23] An expedition was sent from Pittsylvania County to Fort Patrick Henry in Tennessee to confront Lord Dunmore and his Native American allies. As part of this, Captain William Witcher played a crucial role.

"Dressed in hunting shirts and leggins, with their trusty rifles on their shoulders,"[24] William and his company marched through Pittsylvania County before passing through the Blue Ridge Mountains. After his arrival at Fort Patrick Henry, William was told that he was to have one of the most important duties of the war. On October 1, 1776, as the rest of the militia marched toward the Indians villages, William Witcher guarded Fort Patrick Henry. In charge of 200 militia, William was held in high esteem.[25]

While William's militia patrolled the area around Fort Patrick Henry, Native Americans fled before the main army. In their panic, the Indians fled their villages and left their food supply exposed. After

---

[21] Aaraon, *Pittsylvania County Virginia: A Brief History*, 50.

[22] Ray Rapheal, *The First American Revolution: Before Lexington and Concord* (New York, New York: The New Press, 2002), 12; digital images, *Google Books* (http://www.books.google.com: accessed 12 August 2017).

[23] The National Daughters of the American Revolution, *The American Monthly Magazine: Volume XL* (New York, New York: The National Daughters of the American Revolution, 1912), 256; digital images, *Google Books* (http://www.books.google.com: accessed 12 August 2017).

[24] The National Daughters of the American Revolution, *The American Monthly Magazine: Volume XL* (New York, New York: The National Daughters of the American Revolution, 1912), 257; digital images, *Google Books* (http://www.books.google.com: accessed 12 August 2017).

[25] The National Daughters of the American Revolution, *The American Monthly Magazine: Volume XL*, 256.

burning their homes, the English militia agreed to a peace treaty with the Native Americans.

Returning home a war hero, not only had he made his patriotic intentions clear, he also was dissolved from any responsibilities to Great Britain. With the victory over Governor Dunmore and his Indian allies now complete, the judicial system started to change. The expulsion of Dunmore from Virginia also nullified the British legal system.

The culture of Virginia had changed as well. Divided between the Patriots and the Tories, neighbors who were once friends were now enemies. As a member of the committee of safety, William Witcher witnessed tensions rise in Pittsylvania County. Unpopular in southern Virginia,[26] the Tories bore economic penalties under the new government. Seizing their property, American authorities also canceled all debts to England.[27] With their finances in ruins, the Tories held little power in Virginia.

Politically, they were outcasts, especially in Pittsylvania County. Now, required to take an oath of allegiance to the Commonwealth of Virginia, they had to swear to *"renounce and refuse all allegiance to George the Third, King of Great Britain, his heirs and successors, and that I will be faithful and bear true allegiance to the Commonwealth of Virginia, as a free and independent state."*[28]

Elected as a Justice of the Peace on January 1, 1777, William Witcher was now responsible for administrating this oath.[29] Those who refused had their lands taken and sold at auction, nor could

---

[26] M.B. McClellan, *I rode with Jeb Stuart: The Life and Campaigns Of Major General J.E.B Stuart* (Bloomington, Indiana: Indiana Press University, 1958), 4; digital images, *Google Books* (http://www.books.google.com: accessed 13 August 2017).

[27] Stephen M. Millett, *The Scottish Settlers of America: The 17th and 18th Centuries* (1996; reprint, Baltimore, Maryland: Genealogical Publishing Company, 2004), 203; digital images, *Google Books* (http://www.books.google.com: accessed 13 August 2017).

[28] Harry M. Ward, *"Going Down Hill": Legacies of the American Revolutionary War* (Palo Alto: Academica Press, 2009), 19; digital images, *Google Books* (http://www.books.google.com: accessed 13 August 2017).

[29] Larry G. Aaron, *Pittsylvania County Virginia: A Brief History* (Charleston, South Carolina: The History Press, 2009), 53-54.

that person own any guns.[30] As a result, he kept the Tories out of power.

By 1779, Captain William Witcher was again called upon to help in the War for independence. Joined by patriots from the southern American army on June 20, William Witcher and his company began an assault on the earthworks of Stono Ferry in South Carolina. As part of the less, well- trained militia, he was on the front lines.

Ahead of him, William saw cannons stationed behind three redoubts. Behind him, shots from the American light artillery were fired into the cluster of British soldiers. Amidst the deafening sounds of rifles firing, William's men, like most militia, absorbed most of the damage. Noticing the larger cannons of the British plowing down his fellow militia amongst cries for help, General Lincoln issued a retreat.

The battle killed 150 Americans and 129 British.[31] Ultimately, this defeat led to the American defeat at Charleston, South Carolina. However, despite the failure of William to overcome the British, his survival was beneficial to Pittsylvania County.[32]

As the war continued, the economy of the American Colonies suffered. Due to the inflation of the continental dollar, items became more expensive. In 1777, for example, a bag of salt cost $1. However, by 1780, it cost $3,900 dollars.[33]

Pittsylvania County suffered like any another county, but by 1788 William Witcher's new role stablished the economy. With his newly found fame, he became a trustee in a

---

[30] Larry G. Aaron, *Pittsylvania County Virginia: A Brief History*, 53-54.

[31] Lawrence Rowland, Alexander Moore, George C. Rogers, *The History of Beaufort County, South Carolina: Volume 1* (Columbia, South Carolina: University of South Carolina Press, 1996), 223; digital images, *Google Books* (http://www.books.google.com: accessed 15 August 2017).

[32] William Waller Hening, *The Statutes at Large: Vol 10* (Richmond, Virginia: Samuel Pleasants, 1809), 220; digital images, *Internet Archive* (http://www.archive.org: accessed 14 August 2017).

[33] Dale Anderson, *Daily Life during the American Revolution* (Milwaukee, Wisconsin: World Academic Library, 2006), 7; digital images, *Google Books* (http://www.books.google.com: accessed 15 August 2017).

partnership to establish a town called Cooksburg.[34] Among with a few other gentlemen, most notably, Peterfield Jefferson,[35] William stood to gain politically and economically. As a trustee of Cooksburg, he helped stimulate the economy through this new marketplace.

By the time of his death in 1804, William Witcher had lived a fulfilling life. Beginning from his roots as a vestryman, he rose up in society with the intention of helping the community. A lost art in today's world, it was a common practice to be involved with your neighborhood. Despite his early loyalty to Great Britain, he became one of the most influential patriots in Pittsylvania County, Virginia.

Conclusion

The culture of eighteenth-century Virginia in comparison to our modern age couldn't be more different. The community-based ideals of those days are now a tradition long past. However, to study this topic, one can examine the life of Captain William Witcher. Beginning as a vestryman in Pittsylvania County, Virginia, he rose up the ranks of English society. A member of the Established Church of England, his loyalty to the British Government eventually dissolved. As the American Revolution drew near, he was appointed to the Committee of Safety in Pittsylvania County, Virginia. During this time, he served as a Captain of the militia in the southern campaign. After the end of the war, he helped establish Cooksburg in Pittsylvania County to stimulate the weakened economy.

- Beginning on November 15, 1758, William Witcher is recorded in Antrim Parish in Halifax County, Virginia.[36] Tasked with adding new property to the parish, he was responsible for expanding the Virginia Colony.

---

[34] William Walter Hening, *Statutes at Large: Vol 12* (Richmond, Virginia: Samuel Pleasants, 1823), 659-660; digital images, *Google Books* (http://www.books.google.com: accessed 15 August 2017).

[35] William Walter Hening, *Statutes at Large: Vol 12* (Richmond, Virginia: Samuel Pleasants, 1823), 659; digital images, *Google Books* (http://www.books.google.com: accessed 15 August 2017).

[36] Chiarito, Vestry Book of Antrim Parish Halifax County, Virginia, 39.

- As a landowner he purchased and sold land. By June 16, 1764, William Witcher had sold 623 acres of land in Pittsylvania County.[37]

- In 1777, William was elected as a vestryman in Camden Parish in Pittsylvania County, Virginia. Responsible for approving the salary of the minister, processing new land, and providing accommodations for the poor, he had risen in social status.[38]

- Elected as an overseer of the poor in Camden Parish, he oversaw payments that were given to families in need.[39]

- On February 11, 1775, William Witcher was elected to the Committee of Safety for Pittsylvania County, Virginia.[40] Vowing to" *[defend] their liberties and properties, at the risk of their lives, and if required, to die by their fellow suffers [the Bostonians], "* he had taken his first step against the British Government.

- Participating in the war against the Royal Governor, Lord Dunmore on October 1, 1776, Captain William Witcher fought against Dunmore's Indian allies. After this, he was known as a famed Indian fighter.[41]

- Chosen as justice of the peace on Pittsylvania County on January 1, 1777, William had abandoned his allegiance to Great Britain. He was now responsible for administering the Virginia oath of allegiance to Tories.[42] If they refused to accept it, their lands were taken and sold at auction.[43]

- Defeated at the Battle of Stono Ferry in South Carolina, Captain William Witcher and the southern American army were forced to flee. This loss led to the fall of Charleston.[44]

---

[37] Payne, Neil, Payne, *Pittsylvania County Virginia*,19, 135, 137, 182.

[38] Mary Leigh Boisseau, *Vestry Book of Camden Parish (1767-1820)*, (Danville, Virginia: Mary Leigh Boisseau, 1986), 10, 11, 13.

[39] Boisseau, *Vestry Book of Camden Parish,* 51.

[40] Aaraon, *Pittsylvania County Virginia: A Brief History*, 50.

[41] The National Daughters of the American Revolution, *The American Monthly Magazine: Volume XL*, 257.

[42] Harry M. Ward, *"Going Down Hill": Legacies of the American Revolutionary War*, 19.

[43] Larry G. Aaron, *Pittsylvania County Virginia: A Brief History*, 53-54.

[44] Rowland, Moore, Rogers, *The History of Beaufort County, South Carolina: Volume 1*, 223.

- Documented as a founder of Cooksburg in Pittsylvania County in 1788,[45] he had taken a step to stimulate the declining economy. Inflation and a decreased food production had caused a recession.[46] By establishing Cooksburg, he created a new marketplace in an attempt to improve the economy.

---

[45] Walter Hening, *Statutes at Large: Vol 12*, 659-660.

[46] Anderson, *Daily Life during the American Revolution*, 7.

Chapter 8
Sir Francis Wyatt

The Democratic process in Virginia has been a tradition since its founding in Jamestown. Originating from the General Assembly, it was the first legislative body in the New World. This self-governing body which passed its own laws proved to be successful; however, it came at a great cost. Enduring the hardships of oppressive governors, famines, a weak economy, and conflicts with Native Americans, many lives were lost.

By studying the contributions of Sir Francis Wyatt, the first Royal Governor of Jamestown, we can see how this assembly struggled to survive. As governor during the Indian massacre of Jamestown, he was the prime strategist in the war to follow. By today's standards, he is considered controversial; however, he was one of the more popular governors of colonial Virginia.

Sir Francis Wyatt: Born abt. 1588;[1] died at Boxely, Kent, England in 1644.[2] He married Margaret Sandys.[3]

Francis's Parentage: George Wyatt, son of Sir Thomas Wyatt and Jane Finch.[4] She was the daughter of Thomas Finch.[5]

Life Story: The childhood of Sir Francis Wyatt is rooted in the upper class of eighteenth-century England. Born into an influential family, he was

---

[1] Harrison Dwight Cavanagh, *Colonial Chesapeake Families: British Origins and Descendants* (United States: Xlibris Corporation, 2014), 121; digital images, *Google books* (http://www.books.google.com: accessed 19 August 2017).

[2] Cananagh, *Colonial Chesapeake Families: British Origins and Descendants*, 121.

[3] Henry Howard, *The Works of Henry Howard: Works of Wyatt* (London, England: T Bensley, 1816), iii; digital images, *Google Books* (http://www.books.google.com: accessed 19 August 2017); Robert Alonzo Brock, *Virginia and Virginians: Eminent Virginians* (Richmond and Toledo: H. H. Hardesty, 1888), 19; digital images, *Google books* (http://www.books.google.com: accessed 19 August 2017).

[4] Howard, *The Works of Henry Howard: Works of Wyatt*, iii.

[5] Howard, *The Works of Henry Howard: Works of Wyatt*, iii.

raised to be a leader. The grandson of Sir Thomas Wyatt,[6] the leader of Wyatt's Rebellion, and a great grandchild of Sir Henry Wyatt,[7] his lineage was also shrouded in infamy.

Versed in religion and classical literature, Francis Wyatt received a gentile education. Besides being taught Latin, he studied the required ecclesiastical material as well. By now, the Anglican Church had been established as the official denomination of Great Britain. Raised with the belief that an uneducated mind was *"barren and dry,"*[8] he received training to prepare for his future role as governor.

In 1603, at the age of fifteen, Francis Wyatt experienced one of England's darkest times. An outbreak of plague spread throughout England's cities and countryside. As a young man, Francis heard the authorities blame it on society's immorality.[9] It is unknown if he agreed; nevertheless, he managed to survive. As death stalked the cities, Francis was probably isolated in his home in Kent County.

A witness to the attempts of recovery from the plague, he watched the English population decrease. Resorting to prayer, the people begged for forgiveness for their sins in hopes that God would show mercy. As the disease began to fade and hope had once again arisen, so did the functionality of England's institutions.

A couple of years later, he attended Oxford University where he received the best education available.[10] As part of this exclusive establishment, he earned a reputation that was different from his grandfather. These challenging classes provided him with coursework that helped him

---

[6] John Robert Boddie, *Colonial Surry* (1948; reprint, Baltimore, Maryland: Genealogical Publishing Company, 2000), 39; digital images, *Google Books* (http://www.books.google.com: accessed 20 August 2017).

[7] John Robert Boddie, *Colonial Surry* (1948; reprint, Baltimore, Maryland: Genealogical Publishing Company, 2000), 38; digital images, *Google Books* (http://www.books.google.com: accessed 20 August 2017).

[8] Anthony Fletcher, *Growing up in England: The Experience of Childhood 1600-1914* (Connecticut: Yale University Press, 2010), digital images, *Google Books* (http://www.books.google.com: accessed 20 August 2017).

[9] Margaret Healy, *Fictions of Disease in Early Modern England* (Sussex, England: Springer, 2007), 54; digital images, *Google Books* (http://www.books.google.com: accessed 20 August 2017).

[10] Harrison Dwight Cavanagh, *Colonial Chesapeake Families: British Origins and Descendants*, 121.

in his political career. Like his predecessors, he had become associated with the upper class.

Knighted by King James I on July 6, 1618 at the age of twenty-six, Sir Francis Wyatt had risen in society.[11] Considered a person of an "*exalted condition*"[12] he was part of the highest ranks of society. Because of this and his family's lineage, he was now able to serve the crown at the highest level.

On July 24, 1621, Sir Francis Wyatt was appointed Governor of the Virginia Colony. Inheriting a stable economy and a peaceful relationship with the Native Americans, the instructions he received were designed to pursue this course. Although, by modern standards, some of them are now seen as controversial.

Among his most consequential duties was to "*To keep up the religion of the church of England as near as may be.*"[13] A corner stone of colonial society was supporting the Church of England and its policies. As governor of this unified government of church and state, Sir Francis Wyatt knew how this system could lead to discontent.

As the officially recognized church in Virginia, it had supreme political power. Those who were absent on Sundays had to "*forfeit a pound of tobacco.*"[14] Members of the congregation who were absent for a month had to "*forfeit 50 lb. of tobacco.*"[15]

Instructed to "*not to injure the natives; and to forget old quarrels now buried,*"[16] he was required to maintain the peace with the Indians. However, he had a duty to convert Native Americans to Christianity as

---

[11] Harrison Dwight Cavanagh, *Colonial Chesapeake Families: British Origins and Descendants*, 121.

[12] Sir Nicholas Harris Nicolas, *History of the Knighthood of the British Empire* (London, England: William Pickering, Rodwell, 1842), 25; digital images, *Google Books* (http://www.books.google.com: accessed 21 August 2017).

[13] William Walter Henning, *The Statutes at Large: Volume 1* (London, England: Forgotten Books, 2015), 114.

[14] William Walter Henning, *The Statutes at Large: Volume 1* (London, England: Forgotten Books, 2015), 123.

[15] William Walter Henning, *The Statutes at Large: Volume 1*, 123.

[16] William Walter Henning, *The Statutes at Large: Volume 1*, 114.

well.[17] This contradiction proved be a thorn in Anglo-Indian relationships, and led to its downfall.

From an economical viewpoint, he was held accountable. In order to maintain the price and quality of tobacco, he ordered settlers *"not to plant above one hundred pounds of tobacco per head."*[18] Used as tithes to support the English Government, tobacco was seen as a form of currency.

To promote the development of skilled craftsmen, Francis Wyatt implemented a policy to train apprentices.[19] Various trade skills were taught and cultivated overtime, thus strengthening the economy. All types of crafts were encouraged. From blacksmithing, carpentry, and bookbinding, they all became a foundation for expanding the marketplace.

On December 23, 1621, Sir Francis Wyatt issued his first proclamation. Granting *"full power & absolute authoritie, unto Cap*^{t} *William Tucker,"* to *"trade w*th *any Salvages in amitie w*th *us, for Corne or any other Comodities,"*[20] the colony's economy was not yet self-sufficient.

At this time, there was a weakly established peace with the local Native Americans. The Anglo-Indian relationship had improved since the end of the first Anglo-Indian war; however, there was now an unspoken tension. Nevertheless, Indians were free to wonder into English towns to trade. This reciprocal relationship was essential to the survival of Jamestown.

This cooperation between Native American and Europeans, unfortunately, was not to last. Although, it was based on peaceful intentions, Opechancanough, the Pamunkey Chief, planned to betray this trust. Like the older generation of Native Americans, he was worried about the assimilation between the two cultures. A proud believer in his tribe's traditions, he was concerned about Governor Wyatt's plan for an Indian boarding school.[21] Afraid of the example this would set for the younger

---

[17] William Walter Henning, *The Statutes at Large: Volume 1*, 114.

[18] William Walter Henning, *The Statutes at Large: Volume 1* (London, England: Forgotten Books, 2015), 115.

[19] William Walter Henning, *The Statutes at Large: Volume 1*, 115.

[20] Susan Myra Kingsburg, *The Records of The Virginia Company of London: Volume III* (Washington, D.C.: Government Printing Office, 1933), 535-534; digital images, *Internet Archives* (http://www.archive.org: accessed 23 August 2017).

[21] William Walter Henning, *The Statutes at Large: Volume 1*, 114.

generation,[22] Opechancanough intended to drive the Europeans out of the New World.

On March 22, 1622, as trading between the settlers and Native Americans was occurring, there was a hidden plot among the Indians. Without warning, they attacked the western most settlements. Storming the plantations, they killed unarmed men, women, and even children.[23] Those Indians who had been trading and socializing with the settlers had also committed murder with stolen swords, hammers, and other tools.[24]

Sir Francis Wyatt, still in shock, ordered the abandonment of these plantations. The aftermath of this attack led to the downfall of Native Americans on the east coast and to a divided Jamestown. While some people declared that the planters should *bring them [the Indians] to love and reverence the name of that King [of England],*[25] others now saw them as *beasts.*[26] From the viewpoint Governor Wyatt, this tragedy convinced him to implement policies to take advantage of the Indians. As a result, the Anglo-Indian alliance and peace treaty had been broken.

By now, Sir Francis Wyatt had now changed his mind about how Native Americans should be treated. By March 5, 1623 *all trade for corne with the salvages,*[27] was prohibited. Francis even ordered that every house,*shall be pallizaded in for defence against the Indians.*[28] As colonists were ordered to work in the fields with guns by their side,[29] the Royal Governor planned for retaliation.

After the Indian massacre, the outward settlements were initially left abandoned as an illusion. While the English gave the impression that

[22] Janie Mae Jones Mckinley, *The Cultural Roots of the 1622 Indian Attack* (United States: Catch the Spirit of Appalachia, Inc., 2011), digital images; *Google Books* (http://www.books.google.com: accessed 24 August 2017).

[23] David A. Price, *Love and Hate in Jamestown* (United States: Vintage Books, 2003),207.

[24] David A. Price, *Love and Hate in Jamestown,* 207.

[25] David A. Price, *Love and Hate in Jamestown* (United States: Vintage Books, 2003), 209.

[26] David A. Price, *Love and Hate in Jamestown* (United States: Vintage Books, 2003), 210.

[27] William Walter Henning, *The Statutes at Large: Volume 1* (London, England: Forgotten Books, 2015), 125.

[28] William Walter Henning, *The Statutes at Large: Volume 1* (London, England: Forgotten Books, 2015), 127

[29] William Walter Henning, *The Statutes at Large: Volume 1,* 127.

they were defeated, Francis Wyatt was waiting for the time to strike. When the Indian's corn was ripe for harvest he commanded that a series of raids on these fields be commenced.[30]

One can envision English militia burning cornfields amongst the smell of raging fires. Outnumbered, the Indians quickly retreating into the night. In a letter written by Sir Francis Wyatt to the Virginia Company, he describes how one raid brought in,"*a Thowsnade bushel of corne.*"[31] The consequences of these attacks also depleted the food supply of the Native Americans and the English alike.

This desire for corn grew so great that Francis appointed officials to sail up the James River to trade for corn. However, if the Native Americans refused to participate the Captain could "*take it from them by force.*"[32]

On the rare occasion that an alliance was formed with an Indian tribe, Francis would send military assistance to them. The purpose was not solely to help their allies, but rather, it was also to protect the corn supply. On June 16, 1622, this leniency was extended to the "*King of Patomack*"[33] when Captain Isaac Madison provided reinforcements "*against his and our enemies, and to defend them and theire Corne to his Uttmost power.*"[34]

Sir Francis Wyatt became a popular governor because of these now controversial actions. Determined to preserve Jamestown and the general assembly, this was the price he paid. With a majority of the English population killed after the Indian massacre of 1622, it is no

---

[30] William Walter Henning, *The Statutes at Large: Volume 1* (London, England: Forgotten Books, 2015), 123.

[31] Susan Myra Kingsburg, *The Records of The Virginia Company of London: Volume IV* (Washington, D.C.: Government Printing Office, 1935), 9-10; digital images, *Internet Archives* (http://www.archive.org: accessed 24 August 2017).

[32] Susan Myra Kingsburg, *The Records of The Virginia Company of London: Volume IV* (Washington, D.C.: Government Printing Office, 1935), 622; digital images, *Internet Archives* (http://www.archive.org: accessed 24 August 2017).

[33] Susan Myra Kingsburg, *The Records of The Virginia Company of London: Volume III* (Washington, D.C.: Government Printing Office, 1933), 654; digital images, *Internet Archives* (http://www.archive.org: accessed 24 August 2017).

[34] Susan Myra Kingsburg, *The Records of The Virginia Company of London: Volume III*, 654.

surprise that Francis received the support of general assembly.

An advocate for the colonists, Sir Francis Wyatt earned a reputation of applying logic to whatever goal he had. This was especially true when Opechancanough approached the English for a new peace treaty.

In 1623 the Pamunkey Chief requested that a peace be established. Under Governor Wyatt's plan, Native Americans were beginning to starve because of the lack of corn.[35] Desiring to replant corn on their land, Opechancanough released twenty English prisoners as a sign of good faith. The opportunist that he was, Francis agreed, but this was only a deception. Under the command of William Tucker, a group of Englishmen met with the Pamunkey leaders to formally establish this treaty. However, as the Indians drank wine as a toast, they discovered that it was poisoned.[36]

Sir Francis Wyatt had engineered a surprise attack in imitation of Opechancanough's raid in 1622. Many Indian leaders died as a result, but the Chief of the Pamunkey survived. Seen today as a brutal scheme, this along with the other attacks against the Indians helped the colony regain confidence. The lasting, psychological effect of the massacre had left a scar of shame on the settlers. The loss of half its population had threatened its future. However, by 1624 the population and confidence of the colony had been restored, and the "*colonye hath worne owt the skarrs of the massacre.*"[37]

While the Indian population was being reduced due to disease, and a lack of food, Sir Francis Wyatt kept expanding the colony. Forced to "*quit most of o^r habitacons, so that many of o^r people are now unsettled,*"[38] he focused on settling new lands. On June 20, 1622, he commissioned Sir. George Yeardley to explore the Eastern Shore to, "*search for and find out some convenient*

---

[35] David A. Price, *Love and Hate in Jamestown* (United States: Vintage Books, 2003), 218.

[36] David A. Price, *Love and Hate in Jamestown*, 218.

[37] David A. Price, *Love and Hate in Jamestown* (United States: Vintage Books, 2003), 219.

[38] Susan Myra Kingsburg, *The Records of The Virginia Company of London: Volume III* (Washington, D.C.: Government Printing Office, 1933), 656; digital images, *Internet Archives* (http://www.archive.org: accessed 27 August 2017).

*place, both for quantity and quality of ground apt safely to entertaine
some three or foure hundred men,*"[39] to builds plantations.

The founding of these settlements was also rooted in the need to plant
corn, silk grass, sassafras, and other crops necessary for survival.[40]
However, this expansion often came at the expense of the Native
Americans. As European settlers found new areas on which to build
homes on, they intruded on land already owned by Native Americans.
This displacement led to a reduced Indian population and made the
famine worse for the Native Tribes.

Governor Wyatt's and the General Assembly's views on how to govern
were similar. Supporting the Governor's previous decisions on Indian
affairs,[41] they also praised his initiative on expanding the colony. As the
only self-governing legislative body in the western hemisphere, its power
to decide its own fate led to the Declaration of Independence. This form
of government, unfortunately, passed legislation that further weakened
Native American tribes.

By now, Francis had reached his pinnacle of success. Having
stablished the colony's frontier and improved the economy, he became
one of the most popular governors of Jamestown. However, all would
not remain well.

In 1626 Sir Francis received a letter about his father, George Wyatt's,
death in Ireland.[42] Receiving permission to tend to his father's affairs, he
left the office of governor and traveled to Ireland.

This decision had a negative impact on the Virginia colony while also
exposing Francis to the harsh politic situation in Ireland. A supporter

[39] Susan Myra Kingsburg, *The Records of The Virginia Company of London: Volume III,*
656.
[40] Susan Myra Kingsburg, *The Records of The Virginia Company of London: Volume IV*
(Washington, D.C.: Government Printing Office, 1935), 15; digital images,*Internet
Archives* (http://www.archive.org: accessed 27 August 2017).
[41] Susan Myra Kingsburg, *The Records of The Virginia Company of London: Volume IV*
(Washington, D.C.: Government Printing Office, 1935), 102; digital images, *Internet
Archives* (http://www.archive.org: accessed 27 August 2017).
[42] Virginia Historical Society, *Abstract of the Proceedings of the London Company Vol 7
1619-1620* (Virginia Historical Society, 1888), 102; digital images, *Google Books*
(http://www.books.google.com: accessed 9 November 2017).

of the Virginia General Assembly, he was a witness to the collapse of the Irish Parliament and the aftermath that followed.

Like the cultural clash between the English and the Native Americans, Irish politics was riddled with conflict. Divided between the Catholic English Landowners, the Catholic Irish, and the Scottish Presbyterians, tensions were high. While the Scottish planters had taken up lands in the North of Ireland, the Catholic English held onto their valuable land as their influence waned. Deprived of their political power, the Catholic Irish suffered the most.

When Sir Francis Wyatt arrived in Ireland, the Irish Parliament was controlled by the Catholic English; however, the English government eventually striped power away from all three groups. In 1633, Viscount Wentworth was appointed Lord Deputy and began to weaken the Irish Parliament.[43]

Manipulating the parliament in his favor, *"One quarter"* of the land owned by Catholics in Connacht, Ireland was taken.[44] In addition, the Scottish Presbyterians in Ulster were the victims of persecution. Brought before the courts, they were punished for the religious practices they brought from Scotland.[45]

A steadfast supporter of the General Assembly in Virginia, Sir Francis Wyatt learned what would happen if the General Assembly was not preserved. The balance of power between the Governor and the House of Burgesses was the only barrier preventing a monarchy from being established.

During this time, Francis Wyatt learned about the events transpiring in Virginia and the political unrest they was causing. A power clash between the latest Royal Governor, Sir John Harvey, and the general assembly had resulted in revolt. On April 28, 1635,[46] four years before being

---

[43] T. W. Moody and F.X. Martin, *The Course of Irish History* (1967; reprint, Lanham Maryland: Rowman & Littlefield Publishing group, 2001), 158.

[44] Moody and Martin, *The Course of Irish History*, 158.

[45] Moody and Martin, *The Course of Irish History*, 158.

[46] W. Noel Sainsburg, Esq, *Calander of States Papers, Colonial Series (1574-1660)*, (London, England: Longman, Green, Longman & Roberts, 1860), 207; digital images, *Google Books* (http://www.books.google.com: accessed 10 November 2017).

appointed Royal Governor of Virginia a second time, the situation in the colony had reached its climax.

Sir John Harvey viewed the General Assembly's role as advisory and made decisions without their consultation. Under this threat, there was a chance that the King would monopolize the tobacco trade and that the House of Burgesses would be dissolved. The seeds for rebellion had been planted.[47] When a group of rebellious Englishmen were arrested and brought before the Governor's council, "*about 40 musqueteers marched up to the Governor's house*" where Harvey surrendered.[48]

Sir Francis Wyatt must have been distraught after hearing this news. The colony and its form of government he had worked to protect could have been forfeited. However, on January 11, 1639 he was appointed Royal Governor and planned initiatives to improve the economy and punish Sir John Harvey.

The previous administration had left a deep scar on Virginia, so much so that Francis had to once again promote the recovery of the colony. The consequences of the revolt of 1635 had transformed the once stable political situation into a polarized society, one that Wyatt never healed.

During Harvey's administration, the quality of the tobacco crop decreased and, as a result, its price fell. In order to raise the value, Sir Francis Wyatt allowed "*destroying the bad and halfe the goode which was propounded to us.*"[49] This endeavor, although necessary, was also intended to heal the political divide. If the colony could find some common ground behind a strong economy there was still hope.

Another means of attempting to unite the colony was to permit legal actions against Sir John Harvey. Since Sir Francis Wyatt's arrival in Virginia "*They [John Harvey] of the Old Commission have bene persecuted with such malice, the weight whereofe hath hitherto principallye fallen upon Sr John Harvey whose estate is wholly sequestred att p^{rt} sent and att the*

---

[47] Sainsburg, *Calander of States Papers, Colonial Series (1574-1660)*,207.

[48] Sainsburg, *Calander of States Papers, Colonial Series (1574-1660)*,207.

[49] Philp Alexander Bruce, *The Virginia Magazine of History and Biography Vol. 13* (Richmond, Virginia: The Virginia Historical Society, June 1906), 381-382; digital images, *Google Books* (http://www.books.google.com: accessed 11 11 2017).

next Court now approaching will assuredly be swept away."[50] On May 6, 1640, John Harvey himself claimed" *I am soe narrowly watched that I have scarce time of privacye."*

Sir Francis Wyatt also changed his opinion on Native American relations. On January 6, 1639, he agreed to repeal a decision that made it illegal to barter with Native Americans.[51] However, trading guns with Indians was a felony and those who committed this act risked imprisonment.[52]

During the rest of his term, Francis focused on improving the economy by implementing laws that affected all aspects of society. From allowing the resale of wine and liquor, revising how tobacco was traded, and establishing new parishes, he again proved to be popular.[53]

On August 9, 1641, Sir William Berkeley replaced Sir Francis Wyatt as Governor of the Colony of Virginia. Returning to his hometown at Boxeley, Kent, England, he died three years later in 1644.[54]

The death of the late Sir Francis Wyatt marked the end of a troubled time in Virginia. From his first appointment on July 24, 1621,[55] he proved to be an effective, but yet controversial, leader. Pushing the limitations on Native American relations, he promoted the downfall of the Native Tribes. However, despite this, he managed to preserve the General assembly and its independence. In time, this legislative body was transformed into the Continental Congress and became the foundation of the Declaration of Independence.

---

[50] Philp Alexander Bruce, *The Virginia Magazine of History and Biography Vol. 13* (Richmond, Virginia: The Virginia Historical Society, June 1906), 382; digital images, *Google Books* (http://www.books.google.com: accessed 11 11 2017.

[51] William Walter Henning, *The Statutes at Large: Volume 1* (London, England: Forgotten Books, 2015), 224.

[52] William Walter Henning, *The Statutes at Large: Volume 1* (London, England: Forgotten Books, 2015), 225.

[53] William Walter Henning, *The Statutes at Large: Volume 1* (London, England: Forgotten Books, 2015), 226, 228, 229.

[54] Cananagh, *Colonial Chesapeake Families: British Origins and Descendants*, 121.

[55] William Walter Henning, *The Statutes at Large: Volume 1*, 114.

Conclusion

Among the most influential governors of Virginia was Sir Francis Wyatt. Born into a famous royal family, his grandfather, Sir Thomas Wyatt, led a failed rebellion that cast a long shadow over his lineage. From his youth, he received a gentile education against the backdrop of high society. Raised in a family where leadership was valued, he was twice appointed Governor of Virginia. During his first administration, he secured the colony's frontier after the Indian Massacre of 1622. Although, now considered harsh, the methods he used to achieve this came at the expense of Native Americans. After returning for his second term, he was instrumental in preserving the General Assembly and in assisting in the recovery of the economy. By the end of his lifetime, he became one of Virginia's most popular Royal Governors.

- Born abt. 1588 in Boxeley, Kent County, England;[56] he was the son of Sir George Wyatt and grandson of Sir Thomas Wyatt.[57]
- From his youth, he knew about his grandfather's role as leader of Wyatt's Rebellion.[58] Resulting in Sir Thomas Wyatt being beheaded, this cast a shadow over his lineage.
- Raised with the view that an uneducated mind was "*barren and dry*,"[59] he received a gentile education. Among the topics he studied were based on the classics such as Latin and ecclesiastical material.
- A survivor of the plague of 1603, he witnessed one of the darkest times in English history.[60]
- After graduating from Oxford University,[61] he was knighted on July 6, 1618.[62]
- On July 24, 1621, Sir Francis Wyatt was appointed Royal Governor of the Virginia Colony.[63]

---

[56] Cavanagh, *Colonial Chesapeake Families: British Origins and Descendants*, 121.

[57] Boddie, *Colonial Surry*, 39.

[58] Boddie, *Colonial Surry*, 39.

[59] Fletcher, *Growing up in England: The Experience of Childhood 1600-1914*.

[60] Healy, *Fictions of Disease in Early Modern England*, 54.

[61] Cavanagh, *Colonial Chesapeake Families: British Origins and Descendants*, 121.

[62] Cavanagh, *Colonial Chesapeake Families: British Origins and Descendants*, 121.

[63] Henning, *The Statutes at Large: Volume 1* (London, England: Forgotten Books, 2015), 114.

- Charged with keeping *"up the religion of the church of England as near as may be, "*[64] he enforced the strict laws of the Established Church of England. Aware that this was an unpopular endeavor, those who were absent on Sundays had to *"forfeit a pound of tobacco. "*[65]

- On March 22, 1622, concerned over the growing influence of the colony, Opechancanough, the Pamunkey Chief, and his allies launched a surprise attack on the English plantations.[66] Faced with a devastated and crippled raid, Sir Francis Wyatt ordered that the westernmost plantations be abandoned.

- While Sir Francis Wyatt planned for retaliation, he prohibited *"all trade for corne with the salvages."* He also ordered that every house *"shall be pallizaded in for defence against the Indians."*[67]

- When Indian Corn was ripe for harvest, Sir Francis ordered that it be burned.[68] This reduced the food supply and the population of the Native Americans.

- In 1623, Opechancanough requested that a formal peace be established; however, Francis Wyatt had other plans. When Opechancanough and his allies were poisoned at a feast with English diplomats, most of the Indian Chiefs died.[69]

- In the aftermath, Sir Francis allowed the English to settle on Native American land so they could expand the colony.[70]

- After reaching the height of his success during his first administration, he received word of his father's death in Ireland in 1626.[71] Resigning he traveled to Ireland to settle his father's affairs.

---

[64] Henning, *The Statutes at Large: Volume 1* (London, England: Forgotten Books, 2015), 114.

[65] Henning, *The Statutes at Large: Volume 1*, 123.

[66] Price, *Love and Hate in Jamestown*, 207.

[67] Henning, *The Statutes at Large: Volume 1*, 127.

[68] Kingsburg, *The Records of The Virginia Company of London: Volume IV*, 9-10.

[69] Price, *Love and Hate in Jamestown*, 218.

[70] Kingsburg, *The Records of The Virginia Company of London: Volume III*, 656.

[71] Virginia Historical Society, *Abstract of the Proceedings of the London Company Vol 7 1619-1620*, 102.

- A supporter of the General Assembly in the Virginia colony, he witnessed the breakdown of the Irish Parliament and its consequences. This reinforced his viewpoint that a legislative body like the General Assembly was necessary for a government to function.

- Upon the beginning of his second appointment on January 11, 1639, Sir Francis Wyatt inherited a hectic situation. Due to the mismanagement of the previous Royal Governor, Sir John Harvey,[72] Francis was tasked with preserving the General Assembly.[73]

- As punishment for abusing the General Assembly, Sir Francis allowed the estate of Sir John Harvey to be confiscated.[74]

- Passing away in his hometown of Boxeley, Kent, England on 1644,[75] Sir Francis Wyatt had proven himself to be one of the most successful, but yet controversial, governors of Virginia.

---

[72] Sainsburg, *Calander of States Papers, Colonial Series (1574-1660)*, 207

[73] Henning, *The Statutes at Large: Volume 1*, 226, 228, 229.

[74] Bruce, *The Virginia Magazine of History and Biography Vol. 13*, 382.

[75] Cananagh, *Colonial Chesapeake Families: British Origins and Descendants*, 121.

Index

88

www.ingramcontent.com/pod-product-compliance
Lightning Source LLC
Chambersburg PA
CBHW070930270326
41927CB00011B/2793